First published in Australia in 2013 by First Mate Books,
an imprint of Captain Honey Pty Ltd
PO Box 155, Byron Bay, NSW 2481, Australia
www.captainhoney.com.au

Text © Camille Blyth 2013
Illustrations © Sharyn Raggett
The moral right of the author has been asserted.
All rights reserved. Without limiting the rights under
copyright reserved above, no part of this publication may
be reproduced, stored in or introduced in a retrieval system,
or transmitted, in any form or by any means (electronic,
mechanical, photocopying, recording or otherwise), without
the prior written permission of both the copyright owner
and the publisher of this book.

National Library of Australia Cataloguing-in-Publication Data
Blyth, Camille, author.
    The wilderness years : a parents' survival guide / Camille Blyth
    1492895644
    9781492895640
    Child rearing.
    Mother and child.
    Parenting.
649.1

Illustrations, design and typesetting by Sharyn Raggett
5 4 3 2 1   13 14 15 16 17

A PARENTS' SURVIVAL GUIDE

CAMILLE BLYTH

This book is dedicated to each and every woman who wanted a baby but ended up, bewilderingly, with children.

CONTENTS

WHO INVENTED
THE WILDERNESS
ANYWAY?

The Wilderness Years are roughly defined as the time between your first child turning one and your youngest child starting school. The term 'Wilderness Years' was coined when I was consoling a friend who had a four-year-old and two-year-old twins. She was frustrated at having to cancel at the last minute yet another social engagement, and I likened her situation to being cast out into the Wilderness. Life as she once knew it no longer existed and only other parents out there in the Wilderness could possibly begin to comprehend what she was going through. And even in the Wilderness, there were moments when she felt she was the only one out there, surrounded by the endless desolate landscape of child-rearing.

A little in-depth research (asking questions over coffee, change tables and at imaginary tea parties) started to show that there were some very strong, consistent experiences common to all parents (aside from children that is). These experiences seemed to transcend parenting styles, techniques and philosophies and most parenting situations. To put it another way, it didn't matter if you were in a limousine with a driver, or on a tuk tuk with the entire family of 12 balanced on the back, you were still stuck in the traffic, looking at the same gridlock. Sleep deprivation was sleep deprivation, no matter where you were. Vomit had to be cleaned up, wet sheets changed in the middle of the night, toys found...

Just about everyone I spoke to, no matter what their situation, felt alone, exhausted, lost and vulnerable (often all at the same time). They started to believe they were the only parents who spent their nights crammed onto a single mattress with a thumb-sucking, wriggling two-year-old, far away from the marital bed, physically, mentally and emotionally. They thought they were the only parents who couldn't manage basic tasks such as brushing their hair or holding an uninterrupted conversation. The only parents who bickered more consistently and bitterly than warring Afghani tribes. That they were the only parents not coping. They would tramp off to the supermarket with their offspring, feeling like outcasts — no longer members of civilised society. The sensational meltdown by the two-year-old in aisle three only cemented this feeling. It suddenly appeared that online grocery shopping was not that expensive after all.

As the unofficial leader — by virtue of the single fact that my children are a few years older than theirs — of a small but disparate group of parents, I found myself in an unexpected position: a very inexpert expert — simply because I have managed to get most of the way through the Wilderness. (Smell the civilisation!)

I am not sure I have done it very well, or with any particular flair or any notable catastrophes, but I am almost through, and before I forget everything, I would like to leave, for all those who come after, a small gift at the gates of the Wilderness: a Survival Guide. It is there for anybody who would like to pick it up and use it to help them through the next five or so years, or at least it can be used to help light a fire on a damp evening when you feel you have lost your way.

There is a wonderful book called Buddhism for Mothers by Sarah Napthali which you will discover, if you can find some time to sit down and focus, has some really lovely advice. It has a permanent spot on my bedside table. However, in the frantic cut and thrust of day-to-day child-rearing, household running, work, family obligation, dog-walking and laundry, you sometimes need to hear a voice yell across the chaos, IT'S OK, THIS IS NORMAL (please, put that DOWN), TOTALLY NORMAL, AND IT WILL GET BETTER (now, put it down now), AND YOU WILL SURVIVE!

This book is that voice.

WHAT IS THE WILDERNESS?

POSITION VACANT

Personal assistant required to unquestioningly perform all aspects of care for an unspecified number of very unreasonable people.

No formal qualifications required, however, you will need to be highly skilled in the following: macro financing, logistics, diplomatic negotiation in high-pressure, time-sensitive situations, and catastrophe response management. You will also be required to fill the following roles — including but not limited to: Health and Safety Officer, Nurse, Nutritionist, Scientist, Production Manager, Therapist, Entertainer, Chauffeur, Cleaner, Cook, Waitress, Detective, Monster Slayer and Tooth Fairy.

Ability to function with very little sleep, insufficient nourishment and constant negative feedback will be considered an advantage.

The position is full-time with no holiday loading or long service leave.

Car a plus. Immediate start. Salary $0.00 p/a (pro rata).

2383141

Your brain feels like the pantry of the Brady Bunch; it requires vast stocks of nourishing basics and perhaps a few treats. Instead, it has been stocked by a 96-year-old pensioner, and is empty, except for a packet of stale biscuits and a tiny tin of pedigree dog food that is well past its use-by date.

Your skin has seen less moisturiser than Central Australia saw rain during the last drought.

Your clothes are pyjamas, your husband's, or taken from the pile you put away for the charity shop two years ago. Your house looks like yours, except you would *never* let it get so untidy.

You are sitting on the loo, trying to send a text. Your partner, the toddler and the baby are crammed into the bathroom with you: the toddler is helpfully handing you endless bunches of toilet paper, the baby is systematically unwrapping your tampons, and your partner is impatiently asking where his sunglasses and car keys are. You simultaneously pluck the sunglasses and keys from the toddler's 'handbag', remove the remaining three tampons from the baby and hurl them onto a high shelf, and dispose of the toilet paper.

You press 'send' on your text, from which it is clear you are suffering from another bout of cancelitis — a condition that engenders frequent last minute cancellations, usually via text, of any social engagements you made on the basis that things would improve, more sleep would be had, and a babysitter would be available. Note: Conjunctivitis is one of the best cancelitis excuses around — highly contagious and over quickly with no scarring.

Congratulations. The job is all yours!

The Wilderness begins somewhere around the time your oldest child turns one. It can begin earlier and/or with the arrival of a second child — no matter, the deck is stacked and it's stacked against you.

Entire Amazonian forests have been destroyed to produce the amount of paper required to print the vast numbers of books that have been written about how you will cope with pregnancy, childbirth and 'baby's first year'. After that, like the barren treeless landscape, there is nothing but silence.

But it's not just books; even your friends who have children are voiceless. Some say it is a conspiracy of silence. Others see it as a break in the code of sisterhood — your trusted friends who would inform you that your latest boyfriend is a brainless thug, your partner is having an affair with your best mate, or that shade of yellow is not the best colour for your complexion — even they are struck mute. Or could it be that they are just too damn exhausted, busy and confused to have more than a snatched converuption (a conversation that never gets started because of constant interruption by children wanting something) about — well, we'll never know what it was supposed to be about, will we?

No body really thinks about what actually happens beyond the first year of their child's life. Everyone just assumes that things became easier once children can walk unaided, eat unblended food, sleep in their own bed, and dress themselves. Not for one second does anybody think it will get *harder*. In fact, it is around the time the first child is about nine months old that thoughts of a second child really kick in. Do you remember your first child at about nine months old? It is the sweet spot of parenting — a blissful period where a baby is not quite a baby and not quite an autonomous individual.

'Look, Honey, this one is so great, let's try for another,' you say.

'Honey' is more than keen to 'try' for another given the dramatic drop-off in his sex life over the last year. And so, mission accomplished, out come the pregnancy, birth and 'baby's first year' books again...

A child up to the age of one is relatively easy to manipulate. They need food, sleep, cuddles and they generally are happy to do whatever you are doing. Yes, I know that if you are dealing with your first five-month-old that may appear to be an over-simplification. But once a child turns one (or thereabouts) they discover a few significant things at roughly the same time. They discover the ability to move around unassisted, the ability to communicate their needs and wants, and a very strong desire to do these things WHEN AND HOW THEY WANT TO. And there it is, writ large across the gates to the Wilderness — Independent Free Will and the Desire and Ability to Use it.

Resistance is futile multiplied by the number of children you have. Children want. Or they don't want. Or they want both simultaneously. They want you close by, and they want you far away. At the same time. Whatever they want, it's up to you to sort it out. No matter what parenting philosophy you adhere to, what your ideals are, what religion you are, what colour your front door is, you will be forced to enter into endless negotiations over just about everything: which socks to wear, what to eat for breakfast, what will happen if the cat dies, where to go and whether or not pyjamas can be worn for five days straight. Endless negotiation, coercion, deal-making and deal-breaking, all day, every day until you finally break and leave the house with a child who ate a chocolate frog for breakfast and is wearing six-day-old pyjamas. Oddly enough, you will feel triumphant.

THE THEORY OF RELATIVITY

Now you understand that parenting becomes harder, not easier, let's move swiftly onto the next concept. Sir Isaac Newton never married or had children of his own, however if he had, he would have come up with a theory that sounded something like this: 'For every action there is an equal and opposite reaction.' He possibly came up with that anyway...

Here is a quick interpretation of Mr Newton's theory as it applies to parenting.

➤ **Sleep:** In order for the children to get more sleep, the parents will get less sleep.

➤ **Passion:** In order to accommodate the passions of your children, there will be very little time or energy left for passions of your own.

➤ **Personal development:** As your child develops character, your character will be worn down.

➤ **Money:** The more money you need, the less there is.

➤ **Food:** In order to expand your child's palate, you will have to eat cheese sandwiches for about three years.

➤ **Exercise:** So that you can get your children to Gymberoo, swimming lessons and soccer practice, you will spend more time sitting in your car than you thought possible.

➤ **Time to yourself:** They want to spend all their time with you. You want to spend some time with you too — sadly these two things are mutually exclusive.

And finally, the exception that proves the rule:

➤ **Love:** The more love your children need, the more you have to give them.

So the journey across the Wilderness is completely different for parents and children. For parents, it is a bizarre period when all the freedom and character you have cultivated until now has to be put aside. You suddenly find that you are no longer an individual who is able to make independent decisions, indulge in spur of the moment adventures, or read a book in one sitting. You drift further away from who you were and towards a vague misty area populated with dusty old mirrors that give you hints of who you once were, who you might be and... 'HOLY SHIT, WHO IS THAT?'

For children, however, it is a time of vast and exciting discovery. The exploration of new things is a necessary right of passage from babyhood to being a big person who goes to school. More things are learned in these four to five years than any other time in life: how to move independently, how to communicate (both verbally and non-verbally), how to eat, (and how not to eat), what emotions are and how to use them, what all the bits of your body do (and some things they don't do), how to play with other children, basic social skills and the continuous development of their own free will. It is a time of expansion, joy, expression, and discovery. It is ironic that in order for children to fully enjoy this brave new world of discovery, parents have to give up practically everything the children are discovering.

As adults we are told not to sweat the small stuff. For two-year-olds, there is only small stuff, and boy, is it important! Take emotions as an example. A child's response to emotions is similar to their approach to a dress-up basket. He rifles through like a miniature tornado, throwing on the most unlikely combination of garments and becoming psychotically attached to a lurid, acrylic skirt worn as a strapless dress, combined with pink shorts, worn as a hat. He will then insist that he is a) gorgeous and b) ready to go. It's just unfortunate it's your partner's work lunch that he's ready for.

While your children are playing dress-ups with the full gamut of available emotions, glancing at a mirror you find you look alarmingly like the love child of Vivienne Westwood and John Galliano, and you have to search desperately for a breakfast-cereal coloured coat to cover it all up before anyone notices.

So while the children are on an amazing path of discovery and adventure, the parents are forced to endure less spontaneity, less mobility, less stimulation, less sleep, less routine, less time with friends. Less free will. This is the Wilderness. Grab a coffee, (you will never finish it), a sandwich (likewise) and a sturdy pair of shoes. Avoid laces, they are fiddly and time-consuming.

While the Wilderness will continue to be a vast and unpredictable landscape, you will get better at navigating it — more sure-footed the further you travel, and fitter as the years go by. The travel is less related to time, and more to milestones. You will celebrate as you pass the Tree of Toilet Training, The Pillow of Unbroken Sleep, The Rock of Pre-school (also colloquially known as The Ravine Of Heartbroken Mothers Sobbing At the Gate). You will fall into the Whirlpool of Family Illness, only to stagger out weeks later, tired, dishevelled and malnourished.

You will dash off to an exotic tropical location for a family holiday only to find that everyone and everything you were trying to get away from, came with you. Your relationships will be tested more rigorously than the outer tiles of a space shuttle, and you will discover you have a kernel of strength that is both tougher and more brittle than diamond. The first few months in the Wilderness are bewildering, frustrating and depressing. You will feel confused, out of control and exhausted. These feelings will probably not go away for a few years — with any luck you will just get better at managing them.

The good news is that you are not alone! There are millions of other parents on the pilgrimage across the Wilderness. Some you will meet, some you will travel with, and some you will go out of your way to avoid. Like it or not, there are things you will experience that will humble you, humiliate you, and expose parts of you that you didn't know existed — and you thought childbirth was bad...

chapter two

YOU ARE HERE!

The first thing to understand about the Wilderness is that at first it seems a transient place. Everyone is just passing through on their way back to Civilisation and their Old Lives. Nobody — or at least no-one you know — is setting up residency here. It's all mail-forwarding and no permanent addresses. All the other things characteristic of transient communities are present — bed-hopping, damp towels, compromise and more cheap wine and pasta than strictly necessary. Or healthy. Head-lice are not uncommon and sickness is rife.

To be fair, most self-assemble DIY kits of impending parenthood come with a standard warning — you are informed that life will be interrupted, however, after 12 months, normal services will be restored. It may sound like a stopover on a long-haul flight — exotic location, unfamiliar situations — but you have pre-booked transport and accommodation, and it looks like fun. The itinerary assures you that in no time, you will be lining up at customs to get your passports stamped so you can flit off on the next leg of your journey. What you didn't expect was that upon your return to the airport you find the airport has vanished. You are now stuck in a bizarre land, with no apparent way out. You just spent the last of the local currency on a week-old newspaper from a country you will never visit again, so any thought of buying your way out vanishes as well. And just like international travel with a young family, the Wilderness can be fraught with disorganisation. Whose job was it to pack the camera? The first-aid kit? The passports? The tickets? And where the f**k is the itinerary? Tempers are short, and blame is readily available at the Duty Free outlet.

But here you are. And while a relaxed attitude to the journey is ideal, a teething baby and a tricky toddler may quickly use up any equanimity you remembered to pack.

As a parent you battle with the day-to-day chaos of keeping everyone alive, fed and as clean as possible; you also battle with the implications of every decision and action that you take. You grapple with the change in your circumstances and you fret constantly that you won't be able to cope with much more. And yet you do. You draw on the endless well of strength that opened up the moment your first contraction hit. For a moment there it was touch and go as to whether you would survive childbirth, but once you did, you knew, deep down, there was enough mettle to get you through most things. This knowledge will be tested time and time again in the Wilderness and time and time again you will manage to pull it off. Sometimes you will do it with a flourish, other times you will only just scrape in, fingertips bleeding from the final scramble across the line.

One of the main preoccupations in the Wilderness is mastering how to be a Good Parent. It is the overriding goal of the majority of parents and it is a desire that informs and distracts us from beginning to end but the trouble begins with the definition of good parent. Without an official definition from the International Parenting Federation or indeed any official international parenting organisation, it is a concept left to float around like a mist, manipulated by storms, burnt off by sunshine, or coloured by opinion. You will all interpret this concept in your own way. Is it a parent who looks good? Has well-behaved children? Is gentle? Is tough? Pays attention to manners, education, clothing? Or is it the parent who gets the most sleep?

What defines a good parent is up for debate, but the time and mental strength needed for a decent discussion are in short supply out here. You grab the first definition that looks vaguely achievable and dash off in pursuit of a runaway toddler, with a ghost of a plan and a back-pack weighed down with good intentions.

You measure just about everything you do in the Wilderness against the Good Parent/Bad Parent scale. You ask the question, 'If I do this, am I a bad parent?' all the time, but with a special intensity when you are about to do something that is more about you than about your children — a doctor's appointment, or a haircut for example. The big ticket item on the scale is WORK. To work or not to work: full-time part-time, any time that takes your attention away from parenting. For some, full-time work can push the marker down towards bad parent more than part-time work. Some feel that too much television is a bad parent decision. But what if you distract the children with the television because you are making your own nutritious wholemeal spelt pasta? Is the decision then justified? Does the marker rise in the direction of good parent? Subconsciously, you are pushing this marker one way or the other. Of course, you tend to only focus on where the slider is at any given moment, so you don't have the time or space to remember where the slider was a week ago, or work out averages, so you can see whether, on balance, the slider actually spends more time at the good parent end of the scale.

The scale might not be all bad. After all, it keeps you in check, prevents you from giving up entirely on those days when all you have done is dart from one catastrophe to the next and back again. It also holds your sense of righteousness at bay and it allows you a little leeway. It is a self-regulator in a place where regulation is desirable but probably unachievable. Anyway, by the time you reach the end of the Wilderness and wave off your youngest child to school, you realise that the statistics from your Good Parent/ Bad Parent scale won't be analysed for at least two more decades, so you might as well keep your head down and avoid, as much as possible, comparison, competition and your inner critic.

LANDMARKS

There are several significant milestones scattered across the Wilderness. Some are easily recognisable, others are more difficult to discern: a moment, or a feeling. Here are a few obvious ones, but you may have your own list that depends on your unique circumstances.

THE TREE OF TOILET TRAINING

The first time you reach it, it may be an anxious and angst-filled period of time. There are countless books written about this particular task. You can either read them all and choose which method suits you best, read one and make it suit you, or not read anything and hope for the best. Whichever way you choose to tackle this, you will know that someone somewhere did it differently, and while they are heading off down the track with a smug expression on their face, you are standing, inconsolable, with a pair of wet big-boy undies dripping in one hand and a jumbo box of wipes in the other. On the plus side, you may notice a few parents returning from further along with armloads of soiled sheets and fresh packs of pull-ups — they are smiling determinedly and brightly chanting a positive mantra to their children, who are completely unconcerned. You are not fooled by their bravado and may decide to stay right where you are until everyone is confident and ready to move on.

Subsequent visits to the Tree of Toilet Training can either be more or less angst-filled. You are more relaxed about it because you managed it the first time, or much more anxious when things don't go exactly as they did the first time. Experiences like this can undermine your confidence, not just in the matter of toilet training but in your whole fragile belief in your ability to be a good parent.

THE GLADE OF SLEEPING CHILDREN

It was a long night; you have slept in three different beds with three different people, there was no time for a shower this morning and nobody offered you breakfast or a taxi fare out of there. But finally, at 1:30 pm, exhausted by their own nocturnal activities, your house-mates all fall into a deep slumber. One is sprawled across your bed, one on the sofa and the other is, inexplicably, curled up in the washing basket with the clean laundry and a cat for company. You quickly put the kettle on, dash to the bathroom to pee and shower (ALONE!), then quickly put the nursery back into some kind of order. You then decide to risk doing the vacuuming, managing four rooms before your nerve gives out and you decide to tackle the mountain of unfolded washing. After an hour, the only remaining laundry is the pile under the toddler in the basket; you decide to leave it at that and scrub the bathtub instead. Two and a half hours later, you have also cooked dinner, sorted through the massive pile of bills and amassed four bags of clothes for the charity shop. You re-boil the kettle, locate a magazine that is less than six months old and is not stuck together with dried cereal and stale milk, make a cup of tea and sit down... as a high-pitched wail tears through the silence.

It takes years and years of practice to fully understand the Glade of Sleeping Children. Somewhere towards the end of the Wilderness, you will have trained yourself not to see the mess, mentally reorganising your time so you can fold the washing, clean the bathroom and cook the dinner at some other time — next month, for example. You learn to put the kettle on, make the tea and sit down with a book and read it for the ENTIRE TIME THEY ARE ASLEEP. It's a hard-won skill and it should be practised often and with great determination.

THE AGE OF AUTONOMY – A MOVEABLE MILESTONE

The age of autonomy is not around one year old. Many make the mistake of thinking that it is. Sadly, a child's ability to walk does not equate to them cooking their own dinner and washing the car on weekends for extra pocket money. The age of autonomy arrives in a series of moments: sometimes these moments are accumulative, others are singular and isolated. The first time your child gets up, goes to the loo then gets dressed all by themselves might seem like cause for a mid-sized celebration and a bottle of champagne, but don't be fooled: this can be a one-off. They may not repeat this trick again for several years. The same can be said for getting their own breakfast, making their own honey sandwiches and un-stacking the dishwasher.

FINALLY – A FAMILY HOLIDAY!

Despite the fact that your finances resemble a miniature GFC, you have managed to squirrel away a little bit here and a little bit there, and combined with some frequent flyer points, your partner's work bonus and a government handout YOU ARE OFF TO BALI! Words cannot express the feeling of joy, excitement and freedom you feel. You pore over brochures of resorts with lists and lists of fabulous facilities, exotic cuisine and, behold, the Holy Grail of family holidays, KIDS KLUB! In a fervour of expectation, you fill in passport applications for the children. Two weeks later you do it all again, this time taking care to consult their birth certificates for the exact spelling of their names. And then again with the appropriately sized photographs.

Finally, two days before you are due to depart, you have a full set of valid passports, some e-tickets for a budget airline and some bags packed at the front door. The youngest child seems a bit off-colour, however in your fever of excitement, you dismiss it as a common cold and bundle everyone into the car to take the dog to the smart Dog Hotel for his holiday. Kids Klub, Kids Klub, Kids Klub is repeating like a nineties disco anthem in your head.

The night before you are due to leave, the youngest child's common cold has developed into a high temperature and an ear-ache. You make a midnight dash to the closest 24-hour medical centre, beg the doctor for some antibiotics and make it home just in time to bundle everyone into the taxi and head to the airport. After a short delay and a moment of panic at the airport when there seemed to be less children than required, you make it onto the plane to find that only two of the five 'in-flight entertainment units' are actually working and you have left the baby's blankie at home (or in the taxi, but you can't think about that now).

You spend the next six hours stamping out various spot-fires and smiling maniacally at the other passengers. By now you have not slept for 24 hours but it's okay — Kids Klub, Kids Klub, Kids Klub…

Landing and getting through customs is relatively simple because of the assistance given by the very efficient porters at the luggage carousel, and even though your partner looked cross about the cost, you skip out into the heat, unaware that you have been the victim of a basic scam and are short one piece of luggage. But it's all okay — Kids Klub, Kids Klub, Kids Klub…

Finally you arrive at your resort. It is actually a bit smaller than it looked in the brochure, a bit run-down, but there is a pool, a nice cool complimentary drink, and lots of lush gardens with colourful flowers, little ponds filled with fish and the odd turtle. You are still smiling and saying 'thank you' in Thai, despite your partner constantly reminding you that you are in Indonesia. But it's all okay — Kids Klub, Kids Klub, Kids Klub…

You unpack and set out to find somewhere to eat. There is a busy restaurant just along the beach and you find a table and order for everyone. Everybody is hungry — just not for this 'weird food'. The three-year-old pulls out the verbal Kalashnikov: 'Yukyukyuk', but it's all okay — Kids Klub, Kids Klub, Kids Klub …

You finally get everyone fed, back to the room and asleep. You collapse into your own bed and fall into a deep sleep. The following day dawns about an hour after you are woken up by the toddler climbing into bed with you, but you don't mind because today is here and today is … KIDS KLUB!

All you can think of is the sun-lounger by the pool, a series of violently coloured cocktails, a massage and maybe even a beauty treatment. Already you can see yourself at the end of the day, looking like you just stepped out of an advertisement for something really, really glamorous like Riva Speed Boats or real estate in the Mediterranean. You will emerge a beautiful butterfly, no longer the pasty, bumpy slow caterpillar of the last six years. You throw sunscreen over your offspring, get breakfast into them, and sprint off in the direction of the Kids Klub.

Then you arrive. And like a nineties club anthem, there is a sudden screech of needle across vinyl and the beat has gone — suddenly everything is jagged and discordant. The four-year-old holds onto you and refuses to enter the rather dingy-looking building, the baby is sobbing and pulling her ear and the six-year-old deviated to the pool 15 metres ago. Kids Klub. It's not okay. Not at all. Not even by your own desperate standards.

The holiday proceeds to roll downhill from there as you experience a foreign country in ways you just hadn't considered previously. The medical system — for the middle-ear infection. The traffic — to find the hospital. The authorities — because of the accident you caused, and the supermarket — for some food they will actually eat. By the time you are due to leave on the overnight flight home, the four-hour delay due to an industrial dispute by the ground staff barely registers as an issue.

Arriving home you embrace the tarmac like a religious fanatic and vow never to leave the house again.

MAIN ENERGY SOURCE

Another important thing to note is that the Wilderness is fuelled almost solely by emotion. It is true that emotion has been one of the mainstays of civilisation. Without emotion we would be without art, science, passion, wars, peace rallies, Romeo, Juliet, or chocolate. Humans are notoriously emotional. 'I feel' must be one of the most common phrases used, right up there with 'I think'. In the Wilderness, your defences and intellect are so battered by the lack of sleep and all the other bizarre occurrences that all you have left are your emotional responses. And these are raw: like a grazed elbow, there is tenderness at the slightest pressure. You lack the energy or desire to mask what you are feeling and while you can steel yourself against the hysterical sobbing of an over-tired three-year-old, a commercial for a domestic airline will bring you to tears in the opening bars of the jingle.

Like it or not, it is emotions that drive each and every one of us through the landscape of the Wilderness, whether negative, positive, relevant, or irrelevant.

Love forces us from our precious sleep — love for our children and the need to keep them clean, dry, and fed. Sheer desperation can push us further onward, even though every fibre in your body is begging you to give up, check into a five-star resort and book a week's worth of massage, meditation and beauty treatments, right after you have dealt with the mini-bar.

Emotions are like swirling mists: clouds of happiness and fogs of depression with only moments of great clarity. Your emotions will be used by other travellers, by your partner, your children, the help you seek and the help you don't seek. They will also be used by you and the best you can do is try to manage them.

But the main emotion, the foundation and shelter, the source and the end product, is love. It is love that will carry each and every one of you through the Wilderness and deliver you, in relatively good working order, at the end. It is love that flows from the parent to the child and from the child to the parent. It is wise and joyous. It is bountiful and powerful, yet it dances among you like a butterfly.

chapter three

WELCOME ABOARD THE FAMILY BEAST

There is only one form of transport available in the Wilderness. A creature who will carry you, your partner and your offspring from one end of the Wilderness to the other. This creature will start out looking as though he were created by a two-year-old and a nine-month-old using sticky tape, toilet rolls and a wedding invitation. Don't worry, you will get hit with cancelitis before you get to the wedding. As such, he was created with a lot of love, good intentions, and very little skill. He is bound by expectation. He is a beast in the kindest sense of the word — he is big of heart, sound of foot and gentle of eye. He is your Family Beast.

Every Family Beast is a unique, individual character comprised of a number of, well, unique, individual characters! Most Beasts are made up of a mother, a father and assorted offspring. However, there is no set formula. A Family Beast can consist of any number of children who are cared for by two mothers, two fathers, one father and two mothers, one mother or father, a grandparent: any combination really. There is no such thing as an invalid Family Beast.

The Family Beast is above all, your Beast. He is yours to do with what you will. He can be a great hairy unkempt creature, much like a Woolly Mammoth. Or a tame and peaceful bovine Beast with a glossy coat and a slow and steady pace. He can be a dude; he can dance or race or stroll or cavort. Whatever his make-up, his burden is both great and varied, and strength is the virtue best wished upon him. You are an intrinsic part of your Family Beast and he an intrinsic part of you. Over time you and your Beast will become familiar with one another and you will become quite fond and protective of your Family Beast. He's the only one you have got, so it's a good idea to look after him.

You will need to examine your Beast and check that the right components are present and functioning roughly as they should. As a general rule a Beast will have the following basic components: a head, a torso with front and hind legs, and a tail.

THE HEAD
Generally, the smallest, most dependent child sits at the very front of the Head, with all the other children just behind. The Head is the leader — not the decision-maker, but the leader. The needs of the Head will lead the Beast in certain directions. When a new baby arrives, everyone kind of shuffles around a bit to make room, and welcomes them into the group. Babies tend not to make a lot of concessions towards settling in; they just cry a lot and keep the Beast awake.

The Head will inform your decisions in the Wilderness, both on a day-to-day basis and, on a bigger scale, for the future. Food, routines, holidays, sex, friends, sleep, education, the list goes on — and the more children you have, the more complex the Head of the Beast, and therefore The Beast itself, becomes. Throw in things like children with special needs, parents with life-threatening illness, affairs, depression, drug, alcohol, gambling and financial problems (heaven forbid, not all at the same time) and your Family Beast will have a lot to contend with.

THE TORSO

The Torso of the Beast contains all the things vital to survival — such as the heart, lungs, and stomach. The Torso is the domain of the main income earner. For the Family Beast, money is a little bit like air: without it the Beast has a very hard time doing anything at all. Whether we like it or not, it takes money to satisfy the basic essentials of life, such as food and shelter. For the majority of the journey through the Wilderness, it usually falls to one or other of the parents to be the main earner. Which does not mean they are automatically the main spender. In fact, rarely is the earner the spender. The Torso is also in command of the front legs of the Beast, which means decisions about general direction are often made by the Torso.

The Torso is in a difficult position. In today's society, earning money usually means working away from the family for long hours and with a degree of pressure from an employer. In fact, about 80 to 90 percent of the Torso's day-to-day life is totally at odds with the needs of the rest of the Family Beast. They are then expected to be involved in the care and organisation of the children. They are expected to be everything to everyone and nothing for themselves.

THE TAIL

The person who spends the most time and energy caring for the Head of the Beast, resides at the back of the Beast. While there are many fathers now taking up the Tail position, the majority of Tails are mothers. The Tail has the tricky job of making sure the Head of the Beast is happy, healthy and contented, while at the same time, dashing back to the rump to clean up any mess, swat away the flies, kick away any nuisances and then rush back to the Head to break up a dispute, pack lunches and find the missing toy. Never underestimate the power of a bald, smelly soft toy to totally paralyse the Family Beast until it has been found and reinstated to its rightful place, tightly gripped in the hand of the small sobbing person. The Tail is often the one who makes sure there is enough food for everyone and the mortgage or rent and bills are paid (hence the Tail can be the spender). The Tail controls the hindquarters of the Beast and as such has quite a lot of power to determine where the Beast is headed. At the same time, the Tail is so busy they often miss important road signs and billboards as they flick past, only to discover when it's too late that the Beast has come to a cul-de-sac and is turning circles. Fun for the Head, irritating for the Torso and disastrous for the Tail who has to back the Beast up and get back on the right track.

The Tail, in the endless exhausting quest to keep the Family Beast moving in the right direction, tends to ride roughshod over the Torso (who is also stressed and exhausted from providing the fuel for the Beast), leaving the Torso bruised, cross and undernourished.

Because the Tail and the Torso of the Beast have similar positions, although with very different responsibilities, there are times when very little sympathy or comfort flows from one to the other, as each one battles with the sheer volume of tasks requiring completion in order for the Beast to take another step in the right direction. The Tail and the Torso are often locked in battle to establish who has the harder, more overwhelming load of responsibilities. This battle can form a small core of discomfort in the belly of the Beast. This discomfort is generally ignored, occasionally picked up and tossed out, and sometimes left to grow into a large lump of mutual discontent. For the general health of your Family Beast, lumps of mutual discontent are best kept as small and insignificant as possible.

An unbalanced Beast, with back and front legs straining in opposite directions, the Head tossing around and Tail flicking, can quickly become uncontrollable. Often it is up to the Tail of this monster to sort out the mess, calm everyone down and make decisions, however difficult, that are best for everyone involved.

If you feel you have an uncontrollable monster that is crashing around in circles, then there are many places to turn for help and you may want to use them to tame your Family Beast, get your journey back on track and put some joy back into your life. There are community health centres, your family doctor and family therapists, and all will be able to help you, or point you in the right direction. Don't be afraid to use them to help find some semblance of equilibrium, or just get everyone to stand still for a moment so you can all catch your breath.

Modern Family Beasts find ways to combine and divide the responsibilities of the Torso and the Tail, chopping and changing and delineating roles to make the Beast a healthier, happier and more balanced chap, as he carries you all onward through the Wilderness. This takes time, patience, adjustment and above all, the ability to fail and try again. Tails and Torsos will have different ways of looking after the Head. As long as basic principles are adhered to, then the techniques can be different. Mothers mother and fathers father, and each contribute different but equally valuable elements of parenting.

Of course there is no perfect, one-size-fits-all solution — every Family Beast is unique and it is often not until you can see the end of the Wilderness that you will find your Beast fit, healthy, focused and even capable of a playful little skitter. Beware: that playful little skitter can end in a surprise ticket back to the beginning of the Wilderness.

The only thing you can be certain about with your Family Beast is that it will change. Today your Beast may be calm and placid, plodding methodically through the landscape, tomorrow he may be a wild and chaotic Beast cavorting around and heading in completely the wrong direction. Sometimes your Beast will be happy, bright of eye and sharp of step. At other times, his fur will be dull and his heart full of sighs. Accept that your Beast will change, evolve and re-invent himself constantly. Take time to make sure your Beast is fed, rested and loved enough to carry you all through the Wilderness. When you find a sunny glade with a burbling stream, settle the Beast down for a moment, brush the tangles out of his fur, stroke his nose and let him know how important he is to you all. The health of your Family Beast is essential to your journey. Dysfunction, dissatisfaction, disease — all these things will affect the everyday mood and function of your Beast. Very few Beasts are constantly in a calm place of Zen-like harmony, drifting through the landscape on the pure joy of being alive. There may be some who claim they are — but if you follow these Beasts for a while and observe the scats they leave behind, you may be surprised to find things are not exactly as advertised.

The Wilderness is, by its very nature, a slightly unnerving place. Nobody is entirely satisfied with their lot, but a realistic Beast will recognise that while not everybody is getting exactly what they want all the time, most individuals are getting enough to sustain them. The list of things that are generally there, but not in sufficient amounts are: sleep, sex, money, time, freedom, ice cream, chocolate and TV. The things that are there in excess include mess, stress, expectation, guilt, unfolded laundry, and general confusion about what day it is. Despite the imbalance of the load, the frantic activity between the Head and Tail and the lumps of discomfort in the Torso, the Family Beast generally has enough stamina and a cheerful enough disposition to keep moving along, occasionally stopping to have a good scratch and roll in the dust to get rid of some unnecessary baggage.

SPLITTING THE BEAST

Of course there are times when the dynamics of the Family Beast are so out of synchronicity that he becomes totally dysfunctional. At this point, one or the other parent may consider leaving. Splitting the Beast is a messy, sometimes ill-considered event that occurs with alarming regularity in the Wilderness. One of the problems with splitting the Beast is that you can never truly leave the Beast. You are bound to be part of its essence for the rest of your life: not just the rest of the Wilderness but the Rest of Your Life. It gets easier, less intense and, if you are lucky, even fun as time goes on but for the journey through the Wilderness each individual is an integral part of the Beast no matter where you live, how you live and with whom. Which leads us to joining a New Beast.

Joining a New Beast is just as complicated as trying to leave the old one. You are now part of two Beasts, your load more than doubles and your sanity more than halves. Again, over time things become easier or at least more familiar; however, any move to swap from one Beast to another during the journey through the Wilderness should be carefully considered, obsessively planned and above all, involve the Heads of the Beasts as little as possible.

BEAST-LITE

And then there is a Beast with Tail and Torso serviced by the same person. These are lean and focused Beasts indeed. A parent who, for whatever reason, has to do it all is in a difficult position and requires as much help as can be found. There is a great need for a close-knit tribe and an inexhaustible supply of grandparents/relatives/kindly neighbours and teenage babysitters as well as a need for order and routine and organisation.

Death, illness, or divorce can leave a parent in the position of having to fill all the daily requirements of the Beast as well as provide all the emotional support needed. It is a tough journey alone but you will find support; other Beasts will be willing to help out with childcare, dinner or a job that is more family friendly. Be open to the offers and keep taking your vitamins.

BASIC BEAST CARE

It is equally the job of the Tail and the Torso to make sure they are doing the best they can for the Family Beast.

Take a good look at your Family Beast. Look firstly at the Head of the Beast. What needs are there? Which are being met and which neglected? Look at adjusting routines and activities to better meet everyone's needs. Sometimes a good purge is needed to lighten the load — discard some activities, technologies, obligations and general 'stuff'. I have yet to meet a parent who says that adding more of these things to their lives made it easier. Less always means more in the Wilderness (with the possible exception of storage containers and sleep). Have a look at the roles of the Torso and the Tail.

- What are the lumps of mutual discomfort? Dig them out from under the great pile of unfolded clothes in the spare room and examine them together under a bright light.

- Have an honest discussion about how each person feels things are going? Give each person an opportunity to really talk about how they feel. (Try to keep it about your feelings, not their actions — it makes for a nicer discussion.)

- Maybe even write down three things that you would really like to have — time for yoga, a chance to pee without an audience, a holiday in the Maldives — you will all have your own needs.

- Work out a way to accommodate at least one, if not all of these. At a really basic level, break it into blocks of time and trade. Honour each person's block of time and don't abuse the system.

- Acknowledge that the Tail and the Torso are working equally hard under difficult conditions — their responsibilities are different and their work is different, but they both deserve a break.

Over time you will work out your own ways of caring for your Family Beast and which elements require your energy and attention and which ones you can afford to leave. The only real rule is to not neglect him. A neglected and unloved Beast will sicken and even die, leaving a trail of devastation and a really unpleasant smell. And it will probably be left to the Tail to clean it up.

chapter four

COMMUNICATION BREAKDOWN

There are days in the Wilderness when you will wake up to find yourself in the midst of a marketplace. You are surrounded by chaos — noise, dust, stray dogs, and chickens. Your children, like hawkers, are speaking loud and fast in a lingo you think you understand (but hope you don't). Your partner is silently screaming at you, using terms more appropriate to a nearby warring state. You are being sold things left, right, and centre. There are negotiations in progress, but the language is strange, the interpreter is missing and you can't find a phrase-book. The deals being made could be anything from a once-in-a-lifetime bargain to a complete scam. You have no way of knowing if you will end up with a hand-woven rug, a border dispute or a herd of camels.

You tether your Family Beast and calmly, patiently, wait for the cacophony to die down so you can join the negotiations, put in a bid, or get an interpreter on site. But by the time the dust settles, everybody is fast asleep. You have forgotten what it was you wanted to say, and to whom you wanted to say it. Nearby a herd of camels grazes quietly.

Communication in the Wilderness is difficult. Just at the point where your communication needs are at a premium, your children are learning to speak. You re-tune both your mind and your ear to assemble basic sounds into recognisable words. Day in and day out you decipher, discover and direct this emerging lingo, while at the same time you are subconsciously exploring complex and confusing issues within yourself as you grapple with your role as a parent, your sense of identity and your perception of others — not things that are easy to consider when using a language consisting of unformed vowels and missing syllables.

Relationships are linguistic. At the beginning of your relationship with your partner, there is the language of love — the unspoken combination of verbal, physical and emotional communication. You develop together a private dialect, a unique communication used to the exclusion of all others. By the time you reach the Wilderness you will have a fluency that defines your partnership.

The addition of children changes that language considerably. Your children do not learn your language — they re-define the vernacular. They are part of a new relationship, not adjuncts to an existing one. The language of the Family Beast becomes a dialect of a dialect. It is created by you, for you, and it will save you time and time again in the Wilderness. Your dialect contains not just words, but emotion, sign language and body language. Some dialects are poetry, some are great dissertations on love and life, others are complex battle hymns. Your vocabularies change and expand organically, flowing from one need to the next.

The language used aboard your Family Beast is vulnerable to misinterpretation. Once you are in the Wilderness your relationships will change, your vocabulary will change as new words are created and old ones fall from use. Descriptors from your old lives will become meaningless as your journey requires new words, new nouns and verbs to cover the nature of the landscape, the social interactions and the growth of your Family Beast. These linguistic changes can be rapid — an overnight overhaul. Where once you were 'hot', you now fret your children may be too hot. Or they can be gradual — single words taking years to evolve from one meaning to another. The 'barkieboo' emerges as a barbecue, 'magicscene' as magazine. Some just seem to arrive and stick around forever. 'Helisnoopers', and 'helltoes' are possibly helicopters and hotels but you're still not quite sure.

Whatever language you use, you need to be fluent in the lingo and constantly update your vocabulary. The stronger and more confident your dialect, the better it will weather the storms of the Wilderness. When the wind is howling and the thunder is deafening, your ability to lip-read or flick out a message using items of dirty laundry in semaphore signals will be invaluable.

As a mother, you are continually developing ways of communicating with your children but your partner may not always realise that there has been ongoing juggling and pantomime — they have lost their ear for the mother-tongue and are floundering around with a dead language and lots of exasperated hand gestures which can startle the Family Beast, giving everyone a fright.

Some will retreat to a basic Wilderness strategy called 'scheduling'. Borne of necessity, scheduling makes the day-to-day life of your Family Beast smoother and gets everybody where they need to be, with everything they need. Advanced scheduling can also get household duties organised, distributed and attended to.

One of the greatest problems encountered by any language is its vulnerability to misinterpretation and manipulation — something dictionaries can only hope to alleviate. Words are, after all, just words. What give them meaning are all the experiences, emotions and implications that surround them. Additionally there are cultural references, personal translations and pop-culture linguistic graffiti — when a mother says, 'the babe is sick', I can pretty well guarantee it does not mean the same thing it would if her teenage son said it.

A healthy Family Beast will hum with communication; he will be verbally agile and sharply attuned to change. A Family Beast that is linguistically in harmony is a choir with a clear tune that floats around like an aura. That brief snatch of a song leaves you light of heart and strong in your sense of purpose. It drowns out the garbled incoherent babbling that surrounds you like aural housework, and keeps you moving onward through the Wilderness.

chapter five

THE DOG ATE MY RELATIONSHIP

The Wilderness is filled with relationships — with your children, your relatives and friends, your partner, and yourself. As a parent, your relationships with just about everybody will affect your children and inform the relationships they develop with others. As they embark on the journey of building friendships, social groups and partnerships of their own, they are watching you and they are taking notes. Children may or may not listen to the advice you give them, but boy do they take notice of the things you do, and the way you do them. Children are experts in reading undercurrents and in-between the lines; all those things you really don't want them to read. They start by reading our faces as babies and while we might think that speech is the ultimate vehicle of communication, for the first few years babies and toddlers rely on their ability to understand and absorb more intuitive messages and signals. They are finely tuned to the authentic and can spot a fake faster than an antique dealer on Portobello Road.

Your life changes when you have children and this in turn will affect the relationships you have with others — your family, friends, neighbours, bank manager and the phone company. Ties will strengthen, weaken, break, or prove unbreakable. Relationships will change, often evolving from one seemingly static point through some turbulent and unpredictable terrain and on to a new form with new ground rules — effectively a new relationship.

But the most vital relationship you have is the one with the person your children call Daddy.

A relationship is an agreement to journey together. By the time you get to the Wilderness you have usually settled into a companionable step with each other. There are some bumps — occasionally you will step away from each other to get around an obstacle or cross difficult terrain. Sometimes difficult terrain will bring you closer as you help each other. But overall you are in step and confident of your ability to get through most things together. The first 12 to 18 months of travelling as part of a new relationship, a family rather than a partnership, will inevitably test the pace and style of your journey. Most fathers consider it a temporary glitch in the itinerary and they believe they will be back on track shortly. Perhaps you view the Wilderness as a sign that it's over, your baby is growing, and the path ahead will now be smooth and straight. The last thing you expect is that the path will disappear completely and you both will be faced with a wall of impenetrable brambles, strewn with torn clothing and inappropriate footwear. Left with no other direction to follow, you bravely set forth and cut through, with little more than a broken plastic light sabre and sparkly fairy wand to help you.

Emerging on the other side to survey the view — the rolling landscape, vast grasslands, thick wooded hills and mountains shrouded in dense fog — the person who stands beside you appears a stranger. His eyes are wild and hungry, his clothes are not only un-ironed, but unwashed and un-mended as well. He reeks of desperation.

The relationship you have with your partner is exhausted. It is bone weary and malnourished; physically, spiritually and emotionally shattered.

Conceptually, *you* had nine months to adjust to the fact that your relationship is about to be invaded. Your children are of you, they grow inside you, and a relationship develops with your unborn child (or children) over that time. You feel their every movement — you know what affects them and what doesn't. You start to understand who they are. And even if you don't consciously understand what is happening, you strongly suspect the arrival of this child will be slightly different from, say, a puppy or a guinea pig.

Your partner, as empathetic as he may (or may not) be, really has no way of understanding the level of invasion that is about to occur. They can feel the kicks and see the scans, but the first real contact they will have is the rather dramatic birth scene. However they saw you as a person will change. Objectively, how can it not? You made life. And for all their bravado about their superior swimmers and general reproductive prowess, you have done something that defies rational understanding; you have shown a strength that men have been struggling for millennia to replicate. You can steel yourself against the type of pain that nobody has successfully described in any language, in order to deliver the most fragile and beautiful thing imaginable. Life. To generalise, men use their strength destructively — they have had to, otherwise homosapiens would have died from starvation long before humans walked with correct posture. Women use their strength to give life, and men are a bit unsure about who got the better deal. They are in awe of their offspring, and while they may not say it (they may not even understand it) somewhere inside them, they sense that the rules of engagement have changed. They can't change the rules back, and as someone dropped the rule book into the garden mulcher; they are running blind.

Most fathers manage to get through the first year or so with only a few major hiccups. The lack of preparation and understanding of how their lives will change and the realisation that, like a woman's figure, it may never return to its previous state can be devastating. Unfortunately, the person to whom they would normally turn is currently occupied and a little short on time and energy, so fathers can feel excluded — outsiders balanced precariously on the back of the Family Beast, but not actually 'of' the Family Beast.

In those glorious moments when life may have just been created, very few men have the ability to see into the future and gain a glimmer of understanding of how their universe will slip from one cog to another and start spinning on a completely different axis. The transition is seamless — no crunching of gears or obvious changes of pace. Like the proverbial butterfly flapping its wings in the Amazonian jungle, they drift off into a peaceful post-coital slumber, oblivious to what part they have had in creating a future cyclone. Women don't fully understand it at that particular point either but a few weeks of morning sickness tend to spark a realisation or two.

And when the cyclone hits, fathers often find they don't cope well with the chaos. They like order and routine and predictability. It's why they like sport; it looks like chaos, but every week it's the same: there are rules, there is a winner, a loser, a set time, the possibility of some bloodshed, and at the end there is beer.

Children are not like sport. There are no rules: winning and losing is based on circumstance, not scorecards. It is endless, there is guaranteed bloodshed (theirs, yours) and the beer is not for a victorious celebration, but a desperate quenching of a thirst that is, in fact, unquenchable. It is the thirst for a life long-gone, and in the Wilderness fathers will live, or die from this thirst.

Fathers can remain oblivious for several years. The birth of the baby, they are told, will upset life a bit. There will be less sleep, your partner may be preoccupied with the baby for a while, then the advice and literature tails off into nothing — a path leading nowhere. It is testament to the optimism inherent in human nature that we take this lack of information to be a good thing, a positive sign that things will get better: life will return to normal and you can all pick up where you left off a year or so ago. This is what makes the Wilderness more challenging for the fathers — the sheer unexpectedness of it all. Mothers are suspicious. No news is not always good news, mothers know that.

A disconnect in your communications with your partner can throw any understanding you may have into disarray. At the point where you suddenly realise you need some help, someone to lean on, someone on your side, your partner appears to have abandoned you. You didn't expect to be journeying across the Wilderness, but they have been blind-sided, smacked in the side of the head by a curve-ball. Everybody's neediness is like a hunger; it is immediate and non-negotiable. The baby needs daddy, the two-year-old needs daddy; mummy needs help and the dog needs a walk. Daddy needs some peace and quiet, a beer and the Friday night football. Somehow nobody ends up with what they need. You can spend weeks talking to each other, only to realise that the message has been mangled along the way. Trust is compromised and all future negotiations take time, translation, interpretation and more effort than anybody has time for.

Your sex-life is non-existent and sleep is distributed randomly; in fact, the only thing that seems to be available in abundance is resentment and discontent. As you struggle to instil acceptance and love in your children, the most influential relationship in their lives, your and your partners, is under so much strain that it's not something you would want them to be scrutinising too closely. But their antennae are tuned to frequencies you have forgotten even existed and they are listening to just about everything that is not said, which in the Wilderness, is a LOT!

So there you are, a household of beings who either don't know or don't care what emotions are being felt or shown. The only person who may still have a modicum of emotional control is the person who is home the least. But while they get to go out every day and function within civilisation as you used to know it, they must come home to a house fill to the brim with random, unpredictable emotions and needs — an over-tired, over-wrought child and a partner who would like to feel loved and needed — just not by small children and a dog who really, really needs to go for a walk. For some fathers in particular, this can be completely overwhelming and elicit a typically male response — disconnection from the family unit. They will avoid the day-to-day activities of the family and so the great swirling mass of emotions that hits them like a tsunami when they walk through the door every evening. The dog, who at least gets a very long walk, is the only one likely to benefit.

Your children are not accessories to your relationship. Their arrival signals the beginning of a whole new relationship. The quicker you can let go of the old and embrace the new, the easier your journey will be. Some wisdom suggests that you should not allow children to become the centre of your lives, rather look at this new relationship as a circle — all members of the family holding hands, nobody in the middle, nobody on the outside, everybody facing each other.

Too often one parent or the other will feel that they are outside the circle, excluded and shunned, and their desperate attempts to enter the circle are misguided and disruptive. Nobody should be at the centre of the circle unless there is a very good reason for it. For anybody outside the circle, it is important that their intention is to rejoin the circle, and that the circle opens and lets them in.

There is time and space for everybody to take a step in the right direction, but there is no room for one person to take all the steps. The roundness of your Family Beast is a good indication of its health and vitality.

Where once you and your partner had the time and energy to feed your relationship, suddenly there is little time, or inclination to do these things, and when he tries to do something nice for you all you can do is point to the bed and collapse in a sobbing heap. You want to check into a five-star hotel with clean sheets, dry towels, a mini bar full of vodka and chocolate ice cream, and an enormous television stocked full of chick-flicks. And you want to do it ALONE.

It's not that you love your partner any less than you did when you first met, but your head is so stuffed with little snippets of data that add up to the ongoing repair and maintenance of your Family Beast, that there is virtually no space left. Some things will have to last just that little bit longer before needing actual attention. Like a faithful old car that runs on the smell of an oily rag (in fact smells like an oily rag), your relationship is held together with Star Wars band-aids, pink hair elastics and faith. You pray that it can hold on long enough for the children to start school so you can meet one day and go for a walk, talk, even kiss like old times. Except you are so busy with the everyday chaos and catastrophe that you feel you should at least have a quick look under the hood to make sure nothing essential is about to cease. In-between searching for a lost toy and finding a missing shoe, you flick the bonnet up and stare in horror at the void where the engine used to be. You abandon the day's activities, put the children in front of the television and frantically search the internet for a luxury holiday: somewhere that doesn't allow children. After consulting your bank account, which is as exhausted as you are, you have whittled it down to a two-for-one dinner at the local Thai restaurant. You book a babysitter, and a table, and find something to wear. The excitement is palpable.

You settle the children with the babysitter and, practically skipping, you head out with your partner.

Suddenly sitting at the table in the candlelight you find the conversation awkward, worse, even, than a first date. After all, you are supposed to know this man, you have borne his children for goodness sake, and yet…

The babysitter calls to ask what the toddler's 'blankie' looks like and where it might be found, and you both relax and fall into conversation about the children. After an hour you feel your eyes getting heavy and the next thing you know you are being tucked up in bed, with a warm toddler clutching the blankie, snuggled in beside you.

You expected your children to bring you closer, a united 'mum-and-dad' entity who navigate the rolling hills of the Wilderness as one, when in reality you have been left to make all the major decisions about direction, hygiene, and entertainment. While your partner feels as though he is carrying the financial burden of the family, you are left with the mother lode of responsibility. You feel alone with it and you don't even get paid to be abused, ignored and covered in dubious substances.

You want help — someone to wash the dishes at night and hang out a load of washing. Someone with the confidence and ability to take three children to the park for two hours and return with everything and everyone intact. You don't need someone else needing something, asking you to hold the fort for a second longer — you want to walk out the door for an hour and know that everything is going to be okay.

While you struggle to sort out the mountain of unfolded issues in your partnership, you are also grappling with the most important relationship of all — the one you have with yourself.

chapter six

WHO AM I?

Childbirth changes you. No matter what your birth story, it no doubt involved change — physical, emotional, spiritual, and intellectual change. These changes may have started with the actual pregnancy — whatever you thought it was going to be was not exactly what it was. You may have discovered you were having twins, a boy when you wanted a girl, or a girl when you wanted a boy. The baby may have been early, late, upside-down or missing a toe — regardless of who arrived, they did arrive, and they arrived, literally, through you. One way or another, they had to come out. At the end of it all, you were left holding a tiny fragile little being who had just handed over a very heavy emotional suitcase for you to unpack, sort into some kind of order and place on the correct shelves. Only there was no time for that kind of organisation, so the suitcase was left in the middle of the hall for everyone to trip over for the next eight years.

Your interpretation of yourself changes when you have children. Consciously or unconsciously you have expectations. Your perception of who you should be and who you want to be, becomes an unresolvable image that confounds you in much the same way an Escher print might — as soon as you think you have a grip on what is before you, in the blink of an eye, a completely different picture will appear and you are left to adjust your perception again.

The excitement of your previous life burns in your memory as you trudge through the greyness of your domestic fog. Food cleaning washing food ironing folding food washing peace negotiation food cleaning: the monotony is as tedious as it is endless. The pace is set and what remains of your brain is capable only of wiping a runny nose, kicking Lego under the sofa (the volume of stuff that can be stored under a sofa that is only 5 centimetres from the floor deserves a scientific study all of its own) and falling into bed exhausted. The only clue to who you might be was sucked up into the vacuum cleaner a long time ago.

Your identity, who you are, who you want to be and your place in both your own little corner of the world and the world in its larger context is grist to the mill of teenage angst. Establishing your identity can be one of the main pre-occupations of your teenage years, the quest sometimes lasting well into your twenties and early thirties. You spend time, energy (and quite often money) trying to fit yourself into your life, into a tribe and into society. You experiment with personas, careers, travel, cultures and clothes. Roles change as you get older and wiser, and as you move into and out of various relationships.

The role of parenting brings with it another list of things that you may or may not be. What you probably won't be is who you were. Suddenly you realise that that you did know who you were — there were things that defined your character and gave you that special 'you-ness'. But it's a well known fact, 'you don't know what you had until you it's gone.'

And now you have been stripped bare — denuded of all the little things that gave you an identity to call your own.

One of the distinguishing features of your new parenting identity is how narrow your choices have become, and yet you are responsible for broadening the choices your children have. Many of the choices you made in the past have to be unmade; pre-conceptions updated and some hard-won ideals tossed out with the rubbish on Monday night. Your energy is sapped and you have to spread it around the best you can, like the last dollop of butter when there are eight slices of bread to butter — each slice of your life gets a little bit, but by no means enough to make a rich and tasty sandwich.

Your identity was not necessarily a grand gesture, but rather an accumulation of small details, subtle differences and minor similarities, but you were secure in your place. There were hundreds of little things that defined your individuality. You were a wife or a partner. You worked full-time or part-time; played netball on Thursday nights with the girls, drank red wine/herb tea/berry smoothies. You wore heels/flats/trainers/Ugg boots. You had your own style.

And then you are none of these things. Suddenly you are a cog in a contraption that appears to have a mind of its own. Where once you multi-tasked at world-class levels, you now find walking and talking at the same time extremely taxing. Your freedom is impaired, the hundreds of little choices you took for granted disappear, and you are left with a tantruming toddler and a baby with chronic reflux. You are now defined by your children.

You are moving in a new social circle and your children have become your distinguishing feature — like everyone else in the room you are wearing wash and wear clothes, flat shoes and dried cereal on your top. Your hair is tied back in the hope that nobody will realise that it's unwashed. You have donated your signature collection of chandelier earrings to the charity shop and the only accessory you sport is a lanyard with a dummy attached. You frantically scan the room, matching children with mothers so you can get a grip on who is who.

Suddenly this is what defines you. You become 'The Mother'. The mother of little Felix's friend. The mother with the child that bites. The mother of the child in the fairy outfit. While you are in awe of the amazing individuals that you are nurturing, you feel you have been dropped into the big bin of discount home-brand, 'mummies'. You all answer to the same call. You sleep and graze in much the same manner (rarely and inadequately). You have traded style for comfort; your fur is unkempt and your caves are filled with mess, mountains of washing and objects that really, really hurt when stepped on with bare feet. You look at each other in horror, in the realisation that you are all the same. In the great sea of sameness, you struggle to find an identifying feature to cling to as you all swirl together, creating a very sensible shade of brown that hides stains and blends with most interior design schemes.

And with 'The Mother', comes the extension 'A Mother'. There is a certain pitch, a cry that transcends even your radar, which is finely tuned to the cry of your own children. It is the cry of a child in distress. The collective head of all mothers snaps around in that instant, and our primal parental reaction propels us forward. In that moment we are the 'All-mother'. There are women who will lactate at the first cry of a baby. Any baby. In a supermarket. Four aisles away. It is an inbuilt ancient response. It can be buried deep within you, or it can float near the surface, susceptible to every squeak and whimper that reaches you.

There will be days when you huddle under a blanket on the sofa, furtively eating chocolate and praying for divine intervention or a natural disaster. At the same time, your children are breaking out into distinct personalities of their own. They are showing strong preferences for particular clothes, foods, activities and toys, and their choices are rarely the choices you would make. You realise that the last frontier of individuality you had left, has nothing to do with you or your ideals or your expectations, and just about everything to do with theirs. Your children are already consciously starting to set themselves apart from you and from each other in millions of different and, dare I say it, individual ways!

Your identity is also tied to the expectation of the type of mother you thought you would become. The loss of your former identity and the failure to achieve your expected state of parenting can be demoralising, and in a compounding effect, leave you with even less desire to make any kind of effort in either direction.

These are the days when leaving the comfort of your bed requires the kind of effort afforded to running a half marathon. Your body is hungry and malnourished, sapped of all energy. You are so tired that the line between being awake and asleep has all but disappeared; you exist in a zone nestled somewhere between the two. When you do finally drag yourself from under the covers, any thoughts of getting out of your pyjamas defeats you entirely. These are pretty much the rock bottom days of the Wilderness.

But these are not the only days in the Wilderness. There are days of sunshine and enriching hugs and love — these moments can be unexpected and intense. They are the main source of our parenting energy; the fuel that keeps us going comes from these glimmers of hope and possibility. It is the moment of understanding that for the child you hold in your arms, there is no other mother.

There is just one unique you.

chapter seven

YOU HAVE SUPERPOWERS!

Traditionally a superpower is the ability to do something super-human, something powerful and amazing and well, let's face it, impressive! Leap a building in a single bound, walk through walls, turn your enemy into water. In the Wilderness, where superpowers would be useful, what you have is a surprising arsenal of, well, 'anti-powers'. These give you the amazing ability to not do things, but for the sake of morale, let's continue to call them superpowers. You may have always dreamed of possessing superpowers and as you travel through the Wilderness you will discover this impressive set of hidden skills and abilities — each as unexpected as the next.

The Big Book of Superpowers list many of these special Wilderness powers. Here are but a few:

NUMBER 4: JUST. DON'T. DO. IT

The deluxe power-pack version of this superpower will enable you to not do certain things for an extended period of time — three or more years. This superpower is invaluable for those times in the Wilderness where you wonder how you can go on. There is no money, no help, no peace and not a dry eye in the house. Your partner curses you as he steps on a plate of wet paint (at least you hope it's wet paint), then demands higher housekeeping standards, lower noise levels and regular sex. You stay silent, and calmly stack the dishwasher (yet again) while every fibre of your being wants to scream and throw dirty crockery at him. You do this so well the situation immediately diffuses but the boiling mass of emotions you have stuffed away is left to fester indefinitely.

Please note: Of all the superpowers, this is one of the highest consumers of energy — use wisely. Sometimes it's cheaper to replace the crockery, and in extreme cases, the partner.

NUMBER 4A: THE ABILITY TO NOT PANIC

A sub-set of superpower 4, this comes with its own back-up battery pack in case there is a black-out at a crucial moment.

Panic is another intense emotion you learn to control. A panicking mother can put an entire herd of Family Beasts into a stampede. Staying calm in the face of just about any traumatic situation is an essential superpower and should be invoked quickly and convincingly. If you are able to carry on a text conversation with your boss, while speaking to hospital emergency for instructions on how to apply an epi-pen to an anaphylactic two-year-old (and not your two-year-old either), then you have pretty much nailed this one.

NUMBER 7: MANIPULATING THE TRUTH

Parenting is all about truth. Whether you like it or not, you are forced to look at your own truths, your relationships, your situations. But at the same time, you need to guard your truths, you need to assess if a truth is the right one for your children, or if you need to manipulate a truth to better suit the long-term results. Call it lying or call it semantics, the ability to manipulate a truth is an invaluable superpower in the Wilderness and yet not one valued in the real world.

Common examples include:

- 'No, five minutes are not up yet.'

- 'There are no chocolate-chip biscuits in the house.'

- 'Jazz ballet classes are full for this term.'

- 'Of course I would never run away to a tropical island without you.'

As you know, the usual rules so fastidiously adhered to in the real world— truth, justice and the authentic way — are only useful as craft paper out here.

Knowing how and when to use the truth is a subtle superpower, but a valuable one. Like a good chess player, you will develop ability to see far into the future and accurately predict the consequences of the particular truth you are about to impart. If you are especially adept at this, you will be able to remember yourself at 15 and take care with the kind of feedback loop you are about to start. "You promised that I could start jazz ballet when I was seven. You never keep your promises. I wish you weren't my mother." For parents of children who are showing signs of acute memory skills (i.e. any child that breathes), I suggest you master this superpower as soon as you possibly can; it will probably save your life in about 14 years time.

NUMBER 15: FINDING TIME
As you reach the end of your journey in the Wilderness many things will seem easier but time still seems to be in very short supply. We

have worked out how to measure time, but only in relation to itself, our perception of it is distorted somehow. We can set our clocks and time our activities, but time itself stretches and contracts based on an entirely different set of rules. The time it takes a child to reach the age of five can take the standard five calendar years. But on the fourth week of July in their third year when you both have the flu, there is a week that lasts approximately two months. During this period you age about a year. This kind of time/space warp repeats itself over and over and yet, at the end of five years, your child will turn five, and you will wonder where the time went. For the sake of everyone's sanity it is best to ignore what time is actually doing and stick with the clock. If you can develop the ability to manipulate time, it is an amazing superpower to have, but it does requires elements such as acceptance, altered perspectives, and the ability to run really fast. (See Number 34 below.)

NUMBER 21: COMMANDO SENSES
Closely related to common sense, this superpower gives you a skill set not dissimilar to that a Special Forces soldier might graduate West Point or Sandhurst with. These are skills they have spent a significant amount of time and training mastering, but as a mother you simply gave birth and were bestowed with them.

You have five main senses. If one of these is not working — sight, for example — then the remaining senses step in and compensate. Being a mother is similar but instead of removing a sense, you add children. This ensures you develop an additional sense that seems to control the other five, which initially you have no idea how to manage. This sense causes you to fret about your babies. Your normally balanced perspectives are distorted and you overreact to all sorts of perceived dangers and dilemmas. This superpower develops organically as you become more experienced at parenting. And while, by your third child, the baby monitor is nowhere to be seen (or, more importantly, heard), your senses are honed to intuit the slightest change in body temperature, mood, hunger level or degree of mischievousness. Even when you are not actually with your children.

This superpower becomes so much a part of your mothering, you may forget it's even there, until you suddenly sense something, a moment of disquiet a full six seconds before the screaming starts. And then you remember.

NUMBER 34: TORQUE

It looks like 0 to 160 kilometres an hour in less than a second: the speed at which an ambling parent can change direction and leap into highly focused action is really, at this point in time, unquantifiable, but anecdotally it comes under the umbrella of 'very fast', and is similar to the way cats spend their energy. Which isn't a fair comparison, given that cats sleep for about 80 percent of the day.

You will see this superpower in action at night. As your children move towards using night time for sleeping rather than alternate activities, you learn to throw yourself into deep sleep in a manner similar to bungee jumping — quickly, with no time for thought or hesitation. You have no idea how long you will be down or when you will be pulled back up to the platform of wakefulness. A child's wail in the dark of night can pull you up out of deep sleep and throw you into immediate action. There is vomit all over the bed, everyone is wailing and you have tripped on the cat, but even with the baby on your hip, you have dialled the hospital, changed the sheets, poured cups of flat lemonade, and made it back to bed next to your solidly snoring partner in 15 minutes flat. Within seconds, you are bungee jumping back down again.

Rescuing small children from immediate danger is another area where your torque power comes in handy. It is also available for cleaning the house before an unexpected visitor arrives — an entire house can be put in order between the time it takes the visitor to knock and you to call out, 'Be there in a minute'.

If you can possibly take your torque into your life beyond the Wilderness, it will be useful for many years to come.

NUMBER 57: FISCAL GYMNASTICS

'Congratulations on your new child! Here, have a pay rise to compensate for that,' said NO BOSS EVER.

Children don't always mean a cut in the family income, but they definitely mean there are suddenly more outgoings than incomings on the balance sheet. A double income is still possible but the cost of that income can almost cancel itself out. In order to retain at least a modicum of sanity, one or other parent often switches to a part-time paid position (and by default, takes on the majority of the workload). Household budgeting becomes a balancing act that makes Philippe Petit's Twin Tower high-wire stunt look like a cakewalk.

Just about everything goes up. The amount of food, clothes, accessories, health care needs, stain remover and craft supplies multiplies exponentially with the addition of each new child.

Austerity measures will only get you so far. Thrifting is fun until the fourth 1970's clay dinner set pushes the crockery shelf to breaking point, and handmade is creative, satisfying and fine as long as you are not actually leaving the house.

In the Wilderness, fiscal gymnastics are not about budgeting; they are all about charm, wit, being able to sob pitifully on cue, and manipulate the truth (see superpower Number 7). They are also heavily dependent on an acute awareness of dates — disconnection, final warning and payment extension dates. Good fiscal flexibility will see you through but like gymnastics, needs to be practised regularly.

NUMBER 78: LOVE

Your capacity for endless love is, clearly, never ending. There is nobody else in the entire universe who can behave the way your children do — constantly demanding, needing, and draining you — and still be entitled to the love that you have for them. It is the carbon neutral superpower; it's renewable, has no nasty by-products and can be recycled around your Family Beast forever. Superpower Number 78 is the best superpower in the book, and it deserves a better number than 78.

One of the things they forget tell you about superpowers (when they hand them out, willy-nilly), is that they are high consumers of energy. Each time you invoke one of your many powers, you drain your system of energy and you will need a massage, some nourishing soup and an uninterrupted night's sleep to restore you. It is not uncommon to use several of your superpowers in any given 24-hour period, so you are effectively running up a huge energy bill with no conceivable way of paying it back. The fridge is bare, and sleep is a distant memory, occupying the same realm as shoes with heels, manicures and lunch breaks. Unlike a real energy bill, however, there is no reminder letter or disconnection notice to spur you into action, you just keep on spending with no idea how far in debt you really are.

When the day of reckoning arrives and your body collapses in a puddle of un-diagnosable illnesses, you invoke the only superpower you have left (fittingly it is number 283, the last one in the book) and make a doctor's appointment. You pray for enforced bed-rest but you get a 14-day course of antibiotics (followed by the obligatory candida imbalance) and a series of unnecessary and painful blood tests.

While the card at your doctor's surgery may suggest Chronic Fatigue Syndrome, or any number of low to medium grade auto-immune conditions, somewhere in the back of your mind you suspect that you are actually suffering from Common Parenthood and instead of eliminating gluten, dairy or air-born allergens from your environment, you might be better off if you just removed the children for a while.

chapter eight

TRIBAL CONNECTIONS

Tribal behaviour is innate to humans. In the beginning, tribes formed as a means of survival. Given that gunpowder and steel were several millennia away, one small hairless human with no claws or fangs didn't stand much of a chance against a sabre-toothed tiger, but a small tribe of menfolk could overpower a woolly mammoth, then butcher it up into chops and a nice fillet to hand over to the womenfolk to cook for dinner — like gunpowder and steel, feminism was also several millennia away (except for somewhere deep in the Amazon, reportedly). It was survival by weight of numbers.

Ancient tribes consisted of a hierarchy that determined how the tribe would operate on a daily basis. Very broadly, men were the hunters and women the gatherers and nurturers. Within these two groups were those who were better at tracking an animal, some who were better at throwing the spear and those who were better at removing the hide — a group of individuals who operated as a united whole for the better of the tribe. Similarly the women would have fallen into roles specific to their skills and abilities — those who cooked and those who wove and those who nurtured the young.

Even in the animal kingdom — a flock of sheep, for example — there is a small group of ewes who stand guard over a gambolling gang of lambs while the rest of the mob move away for a bit of 'me time'. Somewhere, deep in your psyche, you are constantly trying to replicate this format, albeit in a society that is pulling in a different direction. Organised childcare will do exactly that, care for a child.

But in today's fast-paced world of keywords, catch phrases and linguistic repurposing, the definition of 'tribe' is used more to describe groups of like-minded people. Or people who find themselves in a similar situation at the same time. Like parents.

So while values, priorities, structure and hierarchies change, somewhere among all the technobabble, psychoanalysis, expectation and obligation, you will still manage to find a small herd of Family Beasts who are like-minded, sympathetic to your beliefs, and whose children also have a basic grasp of common manners. This is your tribe.

Your tribe will be made up of fellow travellers who are geographically close (although now that we have means of communications more sophisticated than a conch shell, you can feel close to a very geographically scattered tribe). You will have a code of honour within your tribe that will dictate how tribal gatherings are managed. There will be a certain loyalty and with this there will be cohesion, a knitting together that can, over the years of travelling together, start to felt into a very strong fabric indeed.

At the same time there will be secondary tribes that you are a member of, willingly or unwillingly, and while their support may also have felted into warm, resilient blankets of love, they can also be at war within themselves, or just operate as a loosely woven group with the flow and flexibility of muslin in a breeze: some frayed edges and a couple of holes here and there, some threads stronger than others but, on the whole, holding together.

A FRIENDLY HERD OF BEASTS

Usually by the time you find yourself in the Wilderness, you have formed a strong manifesto for your parenting. A guide for when the undergrowth blocks your path, that also offers reassurance on those bright sunny days when the path is clear and your Beast is trotting along happily. With some measure of luck, manipulation or bribery, you should also have your partner agreeing (at least in principle) with your chosen parenting path.

Your parenting style also forms the foundation of your 'tribe'. They are the group who will be the mainstay of your sanity for the journey. It can be very difficult to travel with a family with a vastly different style to your own. Group holidays are not much fun if half of the group stay in a guest house in the old town, and the other half in the five-star resort on the beach. The Wilderness is much the same. If you crochet organic frittata from handmade wholemeal spaghetti, you are not going to fast-food birthday parties at franchised play-centres with your happy face on. Seek your tribe, have some flexibility (sometimes it's okay not to use organic wholemeal spaghetti) and you will find the Wilderness a much less daunting place. Your tribe will become the bedrock of your existence, you will be intimate with these people in ways you didn't think possible and it's intense and rewarding and essential to your sanity. You will form rituals and routines that will mark the passing of each milestone; there will be simple acts of kindness, and boxes of tissues. Your tribe will offer advice that really is helpful, practical support when needed, and a bottle of wine to share when it all gets too much.

This group may be formed from the mothers you met when you had your first baby. Often these groups stay together for the second and subsequent children. Once you have shared the intimate details of childbirth, passed around feeding advice and secondhand clothes, you will suddenly find you have a tribe. There will also be old friends with children roughly the same age. There are church and community groups, neighbours and the parents you meet at the local park. Your children will start to play a significant role in meeting the people who become part of your tribe, and while this can be a hit and miss kind of process, sometimes having children who play peacefully together is enough to form a friendship. Given the vast range of experiences common to parenting, it is surprisingly easy to strike up a conversation with a total stranger in a park. In a sense it is a little like speed dating — a few pertinent questions and you quickly get a sense of whether someone is simpatico. Or not.

Each member of your tribe will be there for you, in the same way you are there for them. The Wilderness requires a lot of leeway in the relationships that form. Everybody is sleep-deprived, emotionally drained and grappling with the sheer volume of washing that needs to be done every week. Behaviour is unpredictable, often unacceptable, and 98 percent of the time absolutely nothing to do with anything except the nine nights of interrupted sleep, a lack of vitamins and a flat battery in the car. A 'no-frills' bad mood is a good result.

Like all things in life, your tribe will wax and wane and the tribe you started out with will morph over the years into a new tribe, whether the same members are present or not. By definition, journeys involves change, and it is never truer than in the Wilderness. Nothing is static, and although you may feel like you are in a rut, even the rut will change and evolve. One of the nicest things about your tribe is the feeling of acceptance: knowing that nothing you do (well almost) will be deemed unacceptable. There will be moments where beliefs will be challenged and everyone may have to alter their step to accommodate a new idea or situation. Given that separation is rife, illness almost constant and catastrophe imminent, there needs to be constant adjustment. The challenges in the Wilderness are many, varied, and often unexpected and the way we relate to one another can become more intense, the more difficult the situation is. It's good to remember that it's the 'how' that is important, not the 'why', or even the 'who'. How was it dealt with? Was it done with grace and calmness or was it a war-like skirmish that left everyone shell-shocked and bleeding? At the end of the day you have to trust in the strength of your tribe, the honesty of your relationships and keep your expectations in check.

You will also have a genetic tribe. Your genetic tribe will be formed from an assortment of siblings, nieces and nephews, cousins, aunts and uncles, mothers, fathers, grandparents and your non-genetic family — in-laws, stepparents and stepchildren, and adoptive parents.

Your wider circle will encompass ex-partners, a sprinkling of neighbours, and a handful of family friends who have known you since you were born.

The strength of your blood ties will have been set long ago. These ties may be supple and pliable, or time and neglect may have left them brittle and prone to shattering. The Wilderness is a testing time and the strength of your family bond will be strained, strengths exposed, weaknesses found and hidden stress fractures revealed and snapped.

Families are, by their very definition, challenging. Your immediate family have known you since you were born; they watched you grow and consciously and subconsciously, they have affected the way you think, behave and react. The type of person you are now is partly the result of your upbringing and partly the result of who you are — your spirit and your character. Life — circumstances, events, relationships, conditions, culture, religion, environment — creates individuals, who then go on to create more individuals. For some the ties of family are strong and they offer a rich and varied environment for your parenting, bringing to the mix traditional ways of doing certain things — rituals and experiences that have been passed from one generation to the next in a seamless flow of memory, culture and connection. These ties can be threads of spiders' silk that that weather windstorms and cloudbursts.

For others the ties are more fragile. The connections have been weakened or broken over time and distance. They may have been neglected or misused. They could even have been cut. Your genetic tribe, while crucial to the process of becoming who you are, may not necessarily be able to provide the support you expected on your parenting journey.

Often the act of being a parent is cathartic. It can allow you to let go of beliefs and behaviours that are difficult or negative. But sometimes these beliefs remain and continue to define the relationships with your family — both the one who raised you and the one you are raising. There is no correct way to deal with your genetic tribe. Your rituals and traditions will have been set long ago and it is for you to decide what to keep and what to shed along the way. The story of your genetic tribe may unravel behind you as your Family Beast forges forward but at the same time, you have to opportunity to remodel the future as you step into it, adding to your genetic tribal story in ways that could benefit everyone.

Within your genetic tribe, you will have some Tribal Elders: your own parents, now your children's grandparents. It's a good idea to sit under a tree for a moment and see if you can recall your first memory of your own grandparents. Remember your relationship with them. Do you remember it through the prism of your parents' eyes, or do you remember it as one of your first independent relationships?

Grandparents can be a source of great strength: angels who arrive, distract everyone, fold the washing and pop a casserole in the oven. They can be a resource for ongoing childcare or just occasional minding. They offer a wonderful connection between the generations: your children and their grandparents are the bookends of your life. They can offer helpful and hilarious insights into your child's behaviour. Often they can appear baffled by the chaos, time having given the whole catastrophe a nice fuzzy glow. And sometimes they are simply waiting to get their own back! They can be a trusted source of advice, or if they have a completely different outlook on parenting, their advice can be the last thing you want. But when you think that most of our parents saw the beginnings of film, radio, television, mobile phones, computers and the internet, you have to appreciate that attitudes to parenting have probably changed a bit, and look at their advice as interesting anthropological information, rather than something you have to take on board.

Sometimes there are unresolved issues with relatives that need some attention — in extreme cases the best action is to keep away from situations where these are likely to arise, particularly if they compromise the ideals and principles you hold close to your heart. Sometimes the best thing to do is not to be there at all. Only you can decide what is best for your Family Beast, which situations are okay and which are not.

So, alone you are not. Lonely however is another matter … Like a bad dream, you may find yourself entrenched in the wrong tribe. There are a number of ways to end up with the wrong tribe: geography, changes in your ideals, changes in other people's ideals, new members arriving, old members leaving.

Geographic tribes occur commonly in rural and remote areas where there are few options resulting in a herd mentality that is often very singular with very little leeway or flexibility. Being branded an outcast from a situation like this can be a very isolating experience and you are faced with two choices — make the necessary compromises to join the tribe, or go it alone and hope that you will meet up with some more suitable Family Beasts further down the track. Either way you will need strength to carry on.

Sometimes the arrival of a new member to the tribe can alter the dynamic of the group and lead it in a new direction. This can be enriching for everyone or isolating if you feel it's the wrong direction for you. Tribes can split, small fault lines or whole rifts appear, and the herd may break into two or more groups. Like attracts like, and small groups will sometimes join together to create new tribes. It's possibly already been mentioned, but the Wilderness is all about change.

Often the very act of being in the Wilderness can alter some of your tightly held beliefs — about you, the life you want to lead and the world you live in. Your children, by virtue of being your children, have an unnerving knack of re-focusing your priorities, and not just your recent ambitions to eat an uninterrupted meal, finish a conversation and get a full night's sleep. The ambitions and goals of your friends may suddenly seem superficial, very left-wing or right-wing, or just generally on the nose. You find conversations heading off in directions you are just not comfortable with any more. You may think a 4WD is the only safe way to transport your children, that the environment is the crucial issue of the next 20 years, or that private school education as absolutely non-negotiable. Whatever your realisation might be, it's suddenly at odds with your current tribal manifesto and you start to feel as though it's time to duck off down a side path and look for a new herd of Family Beasts to run with.

Despite the complexities of tribal life and the variety and number of tribes, there is one tribe that will emerge as the strongest and most resilient — those Family Beasts that trot along beside you, wait for you if they get ahead and share their fire with you on cold nights. They will carry a child or two for you, as you will carry theirs. Your shoulders will help to carry the brunt of their problems, and your own load will be lightened by kindly hands. The fabric of connection and the wealth of experience from this tribe will be the blanket you use to protect yourself against the harsher elements of the Wilderness.

chapter nine

THE PARENTING GEM

Across time there has been all manner of assistance for parents who feel they are at a crossroads, caught in a maelstrom, or just plain stuck somewhere. There are times when everything seems off-centre and there are disputes, tears, and internal angst. A step in any direction feels wrong, nobody is happy and everything you do seems to just make it worse. The more you search for an answer, the more tangled everything becomes. The sheer range of help can be confusing in itself. Advice comes from everyone from goddesses and deities to psychologists, medicine women and healers. Everything is on offer — from therapy to crystals, essential oils to a good friend with a bottle of wine, herbal tea to a wicked chocolate slice. There is an entire section of books in the library, a sea of relatives, some next-door neighbours, and the helpful girl behind the counter at the health food shop. Your head feels like it's about to implode and your Family Beast is buckling at the knees.

Intuition is a long-recognised phenomenon that has been accepted and rejected at various times throughout history. The subset, mother's intuition, is generally more accepted and understood. Whatever the label, one thing that cannot be denied is the bond that holds a parent and a child in harmony. It is stronger than quick-fix glue, more flexible than bamboo and has more conductivity than copper wire. It is your early warning system, your assurance, and sometimes it is the bane of your life! Intuition originates in your subconscious, arriving as an emotion that has no respect for cold hard facts. Intuition is best described as 'a feeling'; something that niggles away in the depths of your mind, the core of your stomach or at the centre of your heart. Often it is a feeling beyond words, gentle hands softly guiding you in a direction you may not have seen, may be resisting or were not game enough to follow. Intuition often finds you in the middle of the night, in that moment between sleep and waking when your consciousness and subconscious are still a swirling mist of ideas, realisations and imagination. Problems are solved, realities unearthed and ideas break out into your waking world, and what was dark and confusing is suddenly bright, clear and strong. Sometimes it appears in a conversation with a friend, a parent or a professional when something resonates and a sentence will scroll across your line of sight in 24-point bold text: something that makes so much sense you cannot fathom why you didn't see it earlier. It is your intuition, your insight. It gives you clarity and confidences, and strengthens your belief in your mothering.

Your parenting intuition is like a rare crystal — a gem that glows and hums in a luminous flux and vibration so low that with the current bright and shiny lights of information, advice and modern 'wisdoms' you need to sit very still and quietly to connect with it. Your intuition is your knowing. It is your Parenting Gem.

Your Parenting Gem is a talisman that has been passed down through the millennia from parent to child for as long as anyone can remember. The Parenting Gem is a warm and glowing thing. Rare and beautiful, it is unique to you. This Gem is what sets you apart from every other parent out there. It is your essence, your smell, your energy, your touch, your heart.

And while it is your house, your job, your income that you may protect with all the possessiveness of a confused two-year-old, it is your Parenting Gem, the most fragile and vulnerable item bumping around in the bottom of your great big carry-all shoulder bag, covered with sand, grime and tissue fragments, that will help carry you through the Wilderness. With the demise of the wise woman and healer, and as the communal village model of passing information from generation to generation, gave way to the church, the constraints of religion and the bright shiny scientific development of 'Western medicine', the strength of the Parenting Gem dulled as experience gave way to the information and science of the modern age.

You often have little or no idea your gem is there and if you do, you assume it's a cheap crystal from the three-year-old's birthday party treasure hunt. Your Parenting Gem is an invaluable and vital part of the journey through the Wilderness.

There are aspects of parenting that will come naturally; you will feel them in your bones and they will flow like music between you and your children. Anything that comes from your Parenting Gem will be transferred from one to the other with little or no effort. You will all learn and cover incredible distances in a moment.

But of course parenting doesn't always happen like that. There will be rough patches, the path will appear and disappear and you will be left stumbling over dead branches and tree roots in the dark. And it is at times like this that you will most need to consult your Parenting Gem, to follow it and use it as a guiding light.

To be able to unwaveringly follow the warm glowing light of your Parenting Gem is a wonderful and valuable gift that, over generations of parenting, has been relegated to a fourth-tier, low-rent status. Over the centuries, attitudes to child-rearing have swung wildly from one extreme to another. The Parenting Gem has been treasured, misplaced, lost, found, stolen, picked up in a flea market, re-polished, and then left in the back of the Everything Drawer for the last 100 years. Culturally parenting has borrowed, stolen, invented, and given back techniques and styles; it has forced various parenting attitudes upon others. Manners, toilet-training, sleeping, playing, education, entertainment … The net result of all this trading, looting, creating, and imposing is that your Parenting Gem goes missing in all the action. Attachment parenting, nannies, wet nurses, long-day care, and that elusive village needed to raise a child — parenting has run a full gamut of options. It has cross-hatched them with religion, culture and the need to accumulate as much wealth as possible. Materialism has been confused with nurturing, money with love and information with experience. Parenting can be about control rather than observation; information abounds but there is little time for deep learning. Culturally you are reliant on the relentless typhoon of advice, and endless warnings and information. You are becoming suspicious of your Parenting Gem. You second-guess your instincts and you are armed only with your insecurities when you face armies of experts who tell you in no uncertain terms that they know everything you don't, far more about the things you do know, as well as several other things that hadn't even occurred to you. Your vulnerability clouds the clarity of your gem, and constant vigilance and maintenance is required to keep your Parenting Gems glowing and vibrating.

Over time you have been trained to actively seek advice on just about everything, pumping all your vulnerabilities into internet search engines to find out the latest research on every topic from what breed of dog is best for children with allergies, to the schools they will attend to which brand of apple juice has the least additives. You follow prescribed parenting styles and techniques in the same way you would try a new recipe — to the letter, measured exactly and in the correct order, constantly checking to make sure the result looks just like the styled-up full colour photos in the book. You are so concerned with getting it exactly right that you have forgotten that parenting is an individual quest that should, in the end, produce individuals.

In the Wilderness, experts lurk on the most vulnerable corners of the path, waiting to pounce. The experts are smart. They have been doing this for a long time and they have the data to back it up. They know when to target you, with what, and through whom. Is your parenting style the right one, the best one or the most popular? Are you giving your child the right amount of magnesium, the right amount of sun and the right amount of exercise? Are they at the best day-care centre? Are they interacting properly for their age? Do they have the right friends and is a magician an age-appropriate entertainer for a two-year-old's birthday party? Are you subjecting your child to the right kind of plastic, music, learning materials? Do they have enough time with you, and is it the right kind of time? Have you chosen the correct childcare, booster seat, pool fencing, life-partner? Is your child zinc deficient, dyslexic, ADD, ADHD, immunised, able to colour in properly, gluten intolerant, uncoordinated, unmotivated, able to ride a bike without training wheels, having too much TV (or not enough), ready for school or absolutely and totally normal? And are you REALLY SURE?

There is a vast amount of professional advice available in the Wilderness. Sleek offices with modern design, piles of magazines and boxes of toys, all available at a moment's notice to help you with any problem you may have — bearing in mind that a 'moment' can take longer than eight months in the Wilderness. Allergies, behaviours, diseases, the common cold, knock-knees, and obsessions with colour grading the crayons — there is nothing you can think of for which there is not a corresponding professional expert, corrective technique or celebrity opinion. Often, and quite confusingly there are several of each of these, all with opposing advice. But rest assured, given enough time and money they will work to sort out your child's problems. The experts exist because you ask for them. You, with your waning faith in your Parenting Gem, are constantly asking for advice, direction and solutions. It only takes a comment, a question from another parent "Goodness! Is Ali always so active?" to sow the seed of doubt in your mind and you rush off to get an expert opinion.

The reliance on the experts began when you discovered you were pregnant. It can start before that if you needed help to get pregnant. You can delay this reliance to a degree until the baby actually arrives but somewhere along the line, usually when you are feeling vulnerable, a very efficient person will bustle into your life and declare that you need to do something. It may be that you didn't know you needed to do it, or you did but you weren't sure, or you were thinking of doing something else.

It is a brave parent who goes against the advice of her obstetrician, paediatrician, or the draconian midwife on duty the night her milk comes in. From the moment you allow a seed of doubt into the fertile soil of your parenting, you will need to be vigilant, weeding out your insecurities and not allowing them to take over. Some of these seeds are planted by the experts and some of them were planted millions of years ago but, like gills on a bird, they have no purpose for the species you have become.

Food is a perfect example. As part of the planet is in the grip of devastating droughts and food shortages, over here in the First World there is an obesity epidemic. That a child must eat food in order to survive is a small sharp seed, like a bindy, that drives parents to obsess about the food their children are eating. You can be in a constant state of anxiety about your children's food intake. There are books and methods and techniques to make your children eat every imaginable food at the right time, in the right amounts.

Sometimes you forget to stop and look at the bright-eyed energetic children with glowing skin and white teeth that surround you. There is comparison, measuring, weighing and checking and re-checking with a regularity that borders on obsession. It is assumed more is better and while the word 'percentile' fades in the Wilderness, you can easily see whether your child is taller, smarter or faster than the next child. Or not.

The experts trade on possibility. They present all the possible problems and complications that could arise from your inaction, and using the uncertainty they just created, they provide a solution. The net effect is the erosion of faith in your Parenting Gem and subsequent reliance on more experts.

Here are some common areas of angst that have a high expert-to-parent ratio:

SLEEP

Each child arrives with a sleep pattern that is unique to that little individual. The screeching and grinding that can occur as two or more sleep patterns attempt to synchronise can be deafening. And exhausting. For everyone. It becomes an obsession and while sleep-deprived, you are bombarded with information that will 'cure' your sleep woes; information that gives you both hope that there is a cure, and despair when the first 17 methods you try don't actually work.

Eventually, you either stumble upon one that works, or your child grows into a pattern that works with your Family Beast.

TANTRUMS

Tantrums are pretty much non-negotiable in the Wilderness — and by this I mean you cannot avoid them and you cannot negotiate with them. Small children get overwhelmed easily, have little understanding of how to manage their emotions, and they don't have wine so they go into melt-down. They don't save it for behind closed doors or some other more convenient time. But where is the line between acceptable tantrums and excessive, non-acceptable tantrums? If a child doesn't tantrum, are they suppressing their emotions? Justifiably or not, the experts have a huge box of labels that seem to cover just about any expressive behaviour. While generally intentions are well-meant, even some experts are concerned about the rise in the amount of prescriptions issued to children for behaviour-control drugs.

FOOD

Food is big. It's massive. Nutrition, intake, sugar, preservatives, intolerances, allergies, food miles, organic, genetically modified, wholefoods, processed foods, artificial colouring, flavouring, vitamins and supplements. The collective pressure for children to start eating the full range of available foods is huge. Globally our palates are expanding in correlation with the explosion of food-related media we are exposed to. Cooking shows, travel shows, food magazines, food blogs, and recipe apps; never before has there been such an emphasis on the variety of available food. There are shelves and shelves of books dedicated to cooking for your child, making sure they are getting enough of the right foods, how to identify the wrong foods and specialist books for allergies, intolerances and specific food diets. A child that declares they are vegetarian is a blessed relief.

TOILET TRAINING

There are two ways to eliminate waste from the human digestive system, but several thousand guides on the best way to achieve this, when to achieve it and how long it should take to master. It is an area most parents would like to get through as quickly as possible, not least because on the other side there is less expense, less washing and less mess, but sometimes anxiety can hinder rather than help.

Don't be discouraged; there are no teenage-sized nappies in the supermarket.

One thing is certain; most of these things are at the mercy of the attitude of parents. The more a parent can accept — not tolerate or put up with, but truly be 'at one' with, the faster you will be able to move on. Like a car stuck in the mud, the more you rev the engine and spin the wheels, the deeper in you are going. All the help you obtain will make no difference if you don't slow down, find a few points of traction and ease your way forward (or even backwards, because sometimes backwards is really the best way forward) to go on your way again.

At the end of the day, only you will know the best thing for your child and your situation but a good pointer is that if you are feeling confused and frustrated with something and it appears not to be working, then maybe it's time to stop, have a breather and consult your Gem for a bit of direction. In the face of all the information out there, it takes strength and courage to pull out the Parenting Gem, get it glowing again and even wear it boldly around your neck. So when you do, use it to sift through the onslaught of advice and information and find the solutions that work best for you and your Family Beast.

chapter ten

MUMTOPIA V EQUAMUMITY

Mumtopia *(noun)* An imaginary place where you are the perfect parent with a perfect partner and perfect children as defined by the society you exist in.

Equamumity *(noun)* An imaginary state of mental, physical and emotional calmness, composure, and evenness of temper; especially, when dealing with small children, sick pets, and petulant partners.

MUMTOPIA

The biggest culprit in the incessantly unrealistic representations of parenting is the media. The invention of the internet has increased access to a vast range of media. Lifestyle magazines, parenting websites, celebrity gossip magazines, blogs, talk-back radio and daytime television all contribute to the Mumtopia epidemic. The day-spa (where you finally front up for the massage given to you by a well-meaning friend as a birthday gift three years ago) is full of glossy magazines. Each one pinpointing the areas of your life that are just not up to scratch. Beautiful houses, clothes, children, partners and holiday locations are portrayed in such a way that you start to wonder what is wrong with you. Why don't you live like this?

It isn't enough to have to get out of bed, prepare food and care for your offspring, you have to do it perfectly. Every magazine, parenting book and the majority of parenting television programs promote this. Just like the unrealistic body images portrayed in the media for women, and increasingly for men, the concept of 'perfect parenting' is a mirage set just ahead of you in the Wilderness. Society follows general trends: some are helpful, some are not and some have been prevalent for so long they appear to be, deceptively, 'real life'.

In the quest for Mumtopia there is real life and there is actual life. Real life is what life would really be like if your house was nice enough, your bank balance was really big enough, your children and partner really perfect enough, and you could really fit into a pair of size 10 skinny jeans and walk in Christian Louboutin shoes.

And then there is your actual life. Your actual life is what is actually happening right now: the house is a mess, there is rising damp, a falling ceiling and no actual money in the bank. One child has been diagnosed with dyspraxia, the other is eating moisturiser from a cut-price pump pack, your partner has just left for a 10-day surfing safari with six of his mates, and you are still in yesterday's tracksuit.

Neither the quest for Mumtopia nor the search for Equamumity have very much to do with the actual practicalities of parenting. They have everything to do with how your parenting 'looks' to everyone else. We are wired to think that if everything *looks* great it *is* great. My skin is perfect, my clothes are perfect, I am perfect. It is an endless loop: my children appear to be perfect so I am the perfect parent, with perfect children, therefore I am perfect...

To raise children who are healthy of body, mind and spirit is the baseline for parenting. But from the beginning, your choice of obstetrician, midwife, or doula, then pram, sling, and baby seat can be seen as a mission statement for your parenting journey; each one a blatant and unapologetic declaration that this is your path through parenting. For some, it is a way of shouting, 'I will be the best parent. The one with the perfect children and perfect life. I will be the winner'. Designer pram, bigger house, better decorator, larger car, more prestigious school, more glamorous holiday; until certain areas of the Wilderness can begin to resemble a department store boxing day sale at 9:05 am. The point of the 'sale' is lost in the frenzy to grab designer items, regardless of practicality, need, or cost.

The quest to achieve Mumtopia is recognisable from the following scenarios:

➤ The attempt to cook anything with at least 17 ingredients, half of which have been imported from the Middle East, even when you know children will push it off the table rather than eat it.

➤ The attempt to create and maintain a house that is always ready for a *Vogue Living* shoot and features a cluster of children sharing a bowl of fresh raspberries, all dressed in white.

➤ The attempt to not only achieve your 'perfect' body weight, but keep it toned and firm as well. You also try for a wardrobe full of 'current trend' items and shoes with 15-centimetre heels.

➤ The attempt to produce witty duvet covers for the whole family fashioned from a pile of old business shirts and a handy collection of vintage off-cuts left by a great-great-grandmother.

It's helpful to remember a few salient points here.

1) There is nothing wrong with you.

2) The more you know of a person, place or situation, the less 'perfect' they are.

A photo-shoot and an interview give a very, very small snapshot of a very, very small, very, very select section of a person's life. It is highly controlled both by the subject and the medium. There are agendas on both sides, and everyone has their best photo-face on. 'This is my real life!' they are shouting. Nobody feels compelled to admit that their partner dumps their dirty clothes on the bathroom floor and refuses to pick them up, and that their children scream uncontrollably when they are tired and hungry.

Gossip and fashion magazines also tend to feature on the cover every celebrity who ever gave birth to a child, with their miraculous size 0 body proudly on display one week after birth. I am not sure who the people are that run these magazines, but I am even more baffled as to what they might think they are doing. Do they really think it gives us something to work towards? LOOK at these people — they are not real. They have the resources to indulge in expensive cosmetic procedures, personal trainers, and wardrobes that look like a handpicked selection of the best designs from last week's New York Fashion Week.

Victoria Beckham does not see the need to reveal her actual life, nor do the various media outlets who portray her. She is after all, one of their most lucrative celebrities. Victoria Beckham has four children and a husband — she has an actual life — trust me, she really does. She has a Family Beast, she is familiar with the Wilderness. Her life is not perfect.

Actual life is big and messy, cobbled together again with sticky tape and safety pins. In the Wilderness it's magnified ten times. Instead of being a time when you strive for some kind of material perfection, it is far more likely to be a time of resourcefulness — a time to make do with what you have and not get too concerned with what everybody else is up to. It's also a time when it's useful to skill-up on a few things you may never have thought would be part of your life — things like bug analysis, pre-masticated food, and stain removal. You will need to become a medical officer, child behaviour analyst, diplomat, wardrobe manager and garbage man. You will need to improvise at every turn, balance an impossible timetable and a dire bank account with a baby on your hip, as you navigate the battles and skirmishes of daily life. You will need to do it solo, with sinusitis, and all before breakfast.

Any person who has achieved even a modicum of fame (and presumably a degree of financial success as well) and has children feels it is their duty to publicly comment on how difficult it is and how stressed they are and how much their lives have changed. These people often proudly claim not to have any help. Let me explain: no help in the actual world is a mother with a clutch of children, a husband who's working two jobs and no grandparents within a 500 kilometre radius. When celebrities say they have no help, what they really mean is that they don't have a live-in full-time nanny who looks after the children all the time. What they do have is all (or a decent selection) of the following:

- ⤳ A cleaner who comes more than once a fortnight.

- ⤳ A cook/housekeeper who does the grocery shopping, prepares the children's food, helps with the pre-school drop-off and can do the bath/bed routine if required.

- ⤳ A nearby relative who is always available for emergencies and last-minute schedule changes.

- ⤳ A regular nanny/babysitter who is available when you need a haircut, a session with the personal trainer, or an expensive cosmetic procedure.

- ⤳ A gardener who polishes the front gate and trims the lawn with thread clippers.

- A driver. With a car.

- A highly organised assistant who manages all of the above.

But even when you *know* this is the case, the bombardment of unrealistic images is relentless and graphic, so that eventually even the most thick-skinned, centred individual will experience a moment where they start to question their ability to be a successful parent as defined by wealthy privileged celebrities, lifestyle magazines and Martha Stewart. I would argue that it's very hard to get through the Wilderness without actually getting through the Wilderness. There are degrees of difficulty, and most of us don't have time for an uninterrupted coffee, never mind enough time to string a few coherent sentences together in a magazine interview, and pose for the associated photo shoot.

FINDING EQUAMUMITY

Another facet on the prism of perfect parenting is the concept of Zen parenting. This is a neutral mental state supposedly achieved by activities such as yoga, meditation and Ayurvedic diets. It is a state where you can calmly exist with nine children, two dogs, a partner with a monogamy issue, a foreclosure on your mortgage and a car that is totally at odds with your low carbon, sustainable lifestyle goals. The inability to actually achieve a zen-like state while in the Wilderness gives rise to so much angst and frustration. It's enough to make you put on your organic bamboo yoga outfit, curl into bala-asana (child's pose) and sob for an hour before going back to bed, leaving the children to bicker over a box of spelt-flakes and the last drop of soy milk.

Instead you head determinedly into the rest of the day, armed with nothing more than a niggling feeling that you are not quite as centred as you should be. You snap at the children, the woman who queue-jumps in front of you at the bank, and the car key. By the end of the day, your whole body is as tight with tension as a violin string until, finally, you snap, scream at your offspring, throw the Lego box across the room, throw the detox diet out the window and have a glass of wine. Then you worry you won't have time to meditate on the damage you may have wrought on the psyches of your children.

Sometimes tension is the only source of energy you have left; you haven't eaten properly for a week, slept properly for a month, had a single moment to yourself since your first child was conceived and yet you manage to get through each day, organise your children, house and part-time work with enough efficiency to fool just about everybody, except yourself. You can see the fuel gauge; the warning light is on and there's not a service station in sight. You know if you don't soon pull over and re-fuel, the mess you have become will require a post cyclone cleanup strategy, complete with bulldozers, well-meaning volunteers and a structural engineer.

If there is a parent out there who has achieved true Equmumity or Mumtopia, they are keeping very, very quiet and staying well out of sight, eschewing the bazzillions of dollars a 'how to' book would generate. There are many many parents who have truly admirable qualities, amazing strengths and wonderful attitudes to the parenting journey, however it would take quite a few of them, all blended together to even start to come close to the level of perfection many strive for.

Of course, the concept of perfection is in itself imperfect. To start with, it is subjective. There is no definitive measure of perfection. There is 'perfect for now', or 'perfect for me', and 'perfect for you'. There is even 'Perfect. A child has just vomited in my handbag'. However one parent's idea of heaven is another's idea of hell. Parenting is, by its very nature, imperfect. Quite possibly it is supposed to be imperfect. Imperfection creates individuals and it creates uniqueness: flaws are interesting. Imperfection should be celebrated, not avoided.

The failure to achieve a state of Equamumity can result in trauma. The failure to reach Mumtopia will result in the same. This trauma magnifies every parental failure. While it is our nature as humans to strive for a better life, and as parents, to be the best parent we can be, the challenges of the Wilderness are so great that the quest for any kind of perfection should be kicked swiftly under the sofa and left there with the Lego and hair-clips, until some vague point in the distant future. Setting yourself such impossible standards means the distance from their heady heights to your actual life is dizzying. You have given yourself a task akin to climbing Mount Everest without oxygen, a Sherpa or even a pair of socks without holes in the toes.

Hypothermia will be a welcome relief.

chapter eleven

INFLUENCE

As you journey through the Wilderness surrounded by all manner of other parents, each finding their way as best they can, you may notice — provided nobody has stuck a pencil in your eye recently — that each parent represents a battle-zone writ small.

The battle is a low-key, insipid kind of battle. You may not even be aware you are in a war-zone, the victim of direct hits and flying shrapnel. You may be completely unaware of the long and short-term effects. It is a battle against information — it is the war against the Influencers.

An Influencer is anybody or anything that seeks to influence your attitudes and/or decisions. There are two types of Influencer: the Commercial Influencer and the Personal Influencer. The ability to identify and deflect the first and understand the second is a skill that will stand you in good stead in the Wilderness.

COMMERCIAL INFLUENCERS

Commercial Influencers are interlopers in the Wilderness, non-native creatures who have found an endless source of food and water. The more covert and stealthy they are, the less legitimate business they have here.

It is almost impossible, unless your lifestyle is more Amish than aspirational, to avoid marketing. Just about every single thing you encounter in your waking life has been presented to you by a team of marketeers. They include, but are not limited to, the following:

- Graphic designers who are trained to make products and services look as appealing as possible to a specific group of potential customers.

- Copywriters who cleverly use language to create doubt and insecurity and/or desire.

- Public relations companies who know how to use the media to spread information effectively.

- Focus groups who, like survey groups, are only ever as objective as the material given to them.

- Marketing companies who conceptualise campaigns that are as sharp as a needle, aimed with the steady eye of a sniper, and pointed right at you.

And parents are the easiest targets around. We run in herds, we over-share information constantly and we are not likely to stray too far from our group's status quo. We are living under conditions that in any other circumstance would be deemed torture. We are sleep-deprived so our brains are running well below capacity and our emotions simmer on the surface, sensitive to the slightest vibration. Our job is to protect our young, and despite the adverse conditions we do this with the ferocity of lionesses. The Influencers don't take long to realise that the most effective and enduring approach to take is to terrify the socks right off your feet. Termed 'fear-based marketing', it is not even a covert tactic anymore; it is broadly and loudly proclaimed by everyone from the account executives to the stay-at-home mum. It is accepted as normal, combined with an 'expert endorsement', and presented as essential information and advice: Does your child have nits? Asperger's? Flat feet? A strange rash? Breathing difficulties? Trouble with left and right? Are they on the right percentile for their age? Shouting too much? Introverted? Too rough? Are their paints toxic? Is their playground safe and their day-care centre preparing them for school? Are they eating enough of the correct food and absorbing their vitamins…?

The speed at which the range of potential problems grows makes it impossible to list them all, let alone test and diagnose them. In retrospect, the 1970's were not only the last decade of a free childhood, but also fear-free parenting, perhaps because the advertising industry was barely out of nappies itself. Well spoken, bespectacled news readers objectively reported the events of the day on the evening news and nobody was aware of the sheer range of dangers threatening children. Seat-belts were optional, drink-driving was de rigueur, and it was only just dawning on us that smoking might actually be harmful. The 'stranger danger' campaign of the 1970's was one of the first fear-based campaigns created and it was aimed at the children and not the parents, so it didn't induce the collective fear that today's slick sniper attacks generate. Given that relatives, family friends and 'trusted community members' were the worst perpetrators of child abuse, the 1970's 'stranger danger' campaign, while well intentioned, was essentially misguided and probably a waste of resources. In fact today's advertising is often aimed at both parents and children, employing carefully crafted empathy triggers that don't immediately cause any undue alarm. Childhood painkillers are an obvious example — already a shoo-in for parents, with their fast effective relief that offers minimal disruption to hectic schedules (who needs a sick child?), they also sock it to children with a double-barrelled hit of strawberry-flavour and cute-animal-based visuals. And they come in family packs with short expiry dates to boot. Everyone is buying it.

But fear is only one way the Influencers get to us. Another highly successful method taps into our desires. 'Aspirational marketing' feeds our Mumtopia desires.

Aspirational Influencers carefully structure their campaigns, using statistical data, and current trends then add the latest 'true north' of marketing, celebrity endorsement. If you are in any doubt about the power of celebrity, consider for a moment how the Duchess of Cambridge, Princess Catherine (AKA Kate Middleton) can turn an ordinary high-street item of clothing into a must-have item for millions of women all over the globe. Even her sister, Pippa, managed to become one of the hottest items on the face of the earth, just for tagging along at the wedding. (Pippa's bottom sadly sold out some time ago and will not be reproduced, no matter how much you intend to start Pilates next week.) Every single Influencer is waiting to see what pram, baby-gro, baby sling, booties and nursery furniture she will purchase.

Just because something has worked for someone else does not mean that it will automatically work for you, no matter how much you admire or respect that person. Elle Macpherson and Kate Moss look adorable, but — disappointing though this may be — 15-centimetre heels and a Burberry trench coat do not make pre-school drop off any easier. Your child will cry and cling to you no matter what shoes you are wearing, breakfast cereal you have adopted or backpack you have chosen for them.

And while we are under siege, our children are also being attacked. Commercial television is the most common front for the enemy to gain access to our homes and the minds of our offspring, at least before they can read. Like sponges mopping up spilt milk, they absorb images, jingles and colours that have been specifically designed to create an association between the fun experience of a particular advertisement and the corresponding product on a supermarket shelf, a logo on a fast food outlet, or the packaging on a toy. With a complete lack of compunction they formulate a two-pronged attack leaving us nowhere to run and few places to hide.

Overall, the main problem with Commercial Influencers is that once we have followed one, we are susceptible to being influenced by another. It only takes a better marketing spiel, brighter packaging or more frightening information to swing us off in another direction.

Another reason to try something different is because the current product is not working. Unsurprisingly, given that the Influencers main motivation is money, many things are not all they are cracked up to be. Be wary of their approach and the path they are trying to lead you down.

PERSONAL INFLUENCERS

The Personal Influencers inhabit a much foggier area. They are natives: legitimate travellers in the Wilderness. Within your herd, and among your relatives and other family and friends lies a vast store of experiences, ideas and beliefs. You, too, are a Personal Influencer.

Everything that has happened to you, from your own birth to the birth of your children, was in some way preparing you for the challenges of the parenting journey (to be strictly accurate, the ability to drive a D8 bulldozer has only been metaphorically useful so far). Every experience, from warm memories to tender moments that take decades to fade, has marked you in some way. All have helped to form the type of parent you are. Some of these experiences you will draw strength from, others you will rebel against, and some are useful for perspective, as a comparison: 'Hey, I survived childbirth, surely I can get through this.'

The one thing you can't do with the sum total of your experiences, opinions and beliefs is undo them. They are there, they are part of you — they are you.

As Personal Influencers you are generally without a sinister agenda. You are not trying to fleece anybody of their spare change or manipulate them into believing something that is not necessarily in their best interest. In the Wilderness, life is so random and unpredictable you need to surround yourself with as much familiarity as you can. You want to surround yourself with, well, yourself. In the uncertainty of parenting, you want reassurance that you are on the right track, doing the right thing — and if you are not, then at least you are not galloping off in the wrong direction all by yourself.

But while you want to surround yourself with like-minded parents, you don't want them to be exactly the same. You are not looking for a mirror; you are looking for validation. Conversations in the Wilderness rotate around likenesses: 'You are like me and I am like you. I like you.' This is how you end up in your tribes in the Wilderness and it is why you will try (consciously or unconsciously) to influence individuals to be more like you and less like the people you distrust or dislike. It goes back to the tribal mindset and the inherent safety and comfort you have in numbers.

Even if you have lost touch with your Parenting Gem and are making decisions based purely on the information of Commercial Influencers, you look for validation. You are uncertain — are you following the right discipline technique, toilet-training doctrine, education philosophy? You want to know that others are doing the same thing, that it's working for them. It is this validation that keeps your herds together and moving forward with a gentle progression that suits everyone involved.

Innocently or otherwise, Personal Influencers want you to agree with them; after all, imitation is one of the best compliments around. They want you to do the same thing with your children as they do with theirs, follow the same parenting philosophy, join the same playgroup and use the same specialist doctor. It is natural to want to surround yourself with like-minded people. Child-rearing can amplify this need to annoyingly large proportions and the sheer tsunami of information can overwhelm you at any given moment. There are times when you feel you want to wipe the slate clean and start from scratch: a good spring-clean. But, short of amnesia, unknowing something is impossible.

In order to control the relentless onslaught of information, you need to decide what to incorporate into your journey rather than what to extract. Most of us are (due to some genetic programming that happened well before Louis Vuitton created his superb range of luggage for the discerning traveller) chronic over-packers. Why take only one outfit when seven will do? In preparation for your journey through the Wilderness, most of you packed for just about every imaginable circumstance, except for the ones that will actually occur. It is the same with the information that is swirling around. If you ever entirely unload your Family Beast you will find a small reminder branded into his hide 'only take if absolutely necessary'. In order to avoid chronic lower back pain and other disappointments, apply this maxim to all aspects of your journey.

ADVICE

Somewhere, someone will have the key, the vital piece of the puzzle, the link that joins everything together. If you just look hard enough, try all sane options (and in desperation, some insane ones as well), eventually you will find the exact piece of information that will solve your current problem: sleeping/teething/thumb sucking/eating/ crying/bed-wetting, or whatever else is your source of misery. The search can be exhausting; it can cause confusion, angst, despair and exhaustion. You need advice, it needs to be good, and you need it now. You ask friends, experts, relatives, neighbours and the guy who services your car. You read endless books, articles and blogs. Like an investigative journalist you amass all related information. Like a scientist you experiment with different theories, techniques and methods. And then one day you wake up to find that the problem has completely disappeared, morphed into a new problem or split into several problems. You are left with a comprehensive archive of irrelevant data and a severe case of bafflement.

Advice is a river that runs through the Wilderness, a great meandering flow that manages to be within walking distance at all times. It is there when we need it, and it has never run dry in the history of the

Wilderness. It begins high in the mountains where fresh springs of ancient wisdom flow, small tributaries of friends and relatives wind into it and thundering storms of expert advice pour down, swelling the river until the banks are in danger of bursting.

Advice can be invaluable. It can save a Family Beast from tumbling from a cliff-face, prevent a herd from scattering in fright, and generally keep the Wilderness from spinning right off its axis. Advice can also be a source of confusion, and if taken in large quantities over a short period of time can cause stomach cramps.

Every Family Beast carries a canteen with which to scoop up the flowing elixir of advice from the river. It is poured from cup to cup as you pass it around. You tip it out when it becomes rancid, you boil out the impurities, sweeten it with sugar. From the beginning to the end of the Wilderness, you collect, swap, flavour, savour, spill and refill your cups of advice. You start with a great big container. It is heavy and cumbersome and after some time you trade it for a smaller canteen until, by the end of the journey, you have a small hip-flask that you furtively sip from in times of great need. It usually takes the whole journey to understand the power of advice and the delicacy with which it should be handled. You learn to distinguish between quality and quantity. You can scoop up the good advice and leave the bad to flow away, with a small prayer that it will reach the ocean untouched and dissipate.

But while this endless source of advice appears to be authentic, and best of all, free, it can come at a cost.

STORM WARNING

There is yet to be a problem that is without a corresponding book of advice. Somewhere, someone thinks they have the answer. Presented with articulate narratives and witty illustrations, they are difficult to ignore. Especially if they are promising to solve your particular predicament. You want them to solve the problem, you don't want to keep looking, to keep dealing with an untenable situation. You want it fixed, you want it fixed now and you are happy to pay for it. And often, that's just what you will do.

The storm of expert advice fills shelves and shelves of the parenting section of bookshops and libraries all over the world. Parents of every denomination have access to endless literature in every language for every stage of their child's development. They can be written specifically for boys, for girls, for twins, for single children, for children of broken homes, mixed homes, war zones and middle-class, middle-sized families. Food, toilet training, sleeping, behaviour, death, divorce, moving house, Asperger's, asthma, fear of dogs, and allergies: it's all there in hard-cover, soft-cover, talking books and eBooks, and if not, it's coming to a library near you soon. They can come to you fresh from the bookshop, crisp with promise; from friends, crisp with dried food; from relatives, crackling with reproach; or from the shelves of the local library, worn ragged with hope.

They are authoritative, full of promise and often funny. They describe your problem, right down to the last exclamation mark, and then chart a way out of the quagmire. There are detailed instructions and links to helpful websites and communities of similarly beleaguered Beasts. However they come to you, they will do one of the following things:

a) Solve the problem.

b) Exacerbate the problem.

c) Create new problems.

Your relationship with advice is directly related to your relationship with your Parenting Gem. The stronger and brighter your Parenting

Gem, the less you will need to fill your cup from the river of advice. Using the indigenous technique of hydration, you can pop your Parenting Gem into your mouth and suck on it, staving off thirst for quite some time. If your Gem is lost somewhere in the detritus of your life, you may require frequent trips to the river to fill your canteens. And the more you drink, the more you will need to drink.

Expert advice is only part of the make-up of the river. You share your own advice generously. You will share it with your close friends, relatives and parents you meet in the park. You want to help your fellow travellers — you know the Wilderness is a disorienting and confusing place. There are no street lights and no sign posts. There is no roadside assistance, and by the sheer volume of abandoned EPIRB-like devices lying around, you are fairly sure an emergency air-lift to safety is not an option. Kindness is your best bet. You understand the full implications of sleep deprivation or the frustration of a child who won't eat, and you don't want anyone to suffer unnecessarily. You want to help, so you pour your advice into any available receptacle and make sure it is swallowed down with a good dollop of anecdotal evidence of success. As recipients of this advice, you gratefully gulp everything down, digesting any old shred of hope, no matter how recycled it is.

The closer to the end of the Wilderness you travel, the less advice you will need. You see the river for what it is — a great muddy soup of just about anything anybody thought might work, including what did work and what didn't. The labour needed to distil the liquid into its base components is so overwhelmingly complex and time-consuming, it would require a special government department and an advisory board of experts who, quite frankly, have more important things to do.

Time and experience will have taught you not to hand your advice around like champagne at a party. You have learned to keep it close and treasure your wisdom, understanding that it has been distilled from the challenges, the distance and the tears of your journey. You have discovered where to find the good advice in the pools and eddies hidden by overhanging branches, and you carefully siphon small thimbles of it into your lives. You pass it on only when asked and you keep your counsel when not.

OPINION

In addition to all the sources of advice filling the river, there is an increasing number of streams of opinion that feed into it. Never before in the history of parenting has the dissemination of opinion been so prolific, or so easy to do. Blogs, social media sites and websites written by experts, journalists and parents trickle endlessly into the river. And attached to each opinion is a trail of bubbles both agreeing and disagreeing with the stated opinion.

The difference between sage advice and random opinion becomes less and less clear the more they swirl around in the current of the river. As an open forum, the Internet provides a literal free-for-all. Issues are hotly debated time and time again. Science, expertise, studies and surveys are all called into play as each person tries to support a point-of-view. While your virtual tribe can help you continue along your chosen path, even if your actual tribe is not quite in step with you, you need to beware of all the opinions drifting around - they can be vague and personal or borderline fundamentalist with a slathering of generalities. They can be masked as truth or used to dismiss what might be perfectly solid information.

Comments on blogs and websites are usually well written and well argued. The topic will determine the tone of the response. 'Opinion hotspots', including breast-feeding versus bottle-feeding, immunisation versus non-immunisation and childcare versus home care, can incite quite fierce battles. These topics tend to be some of the most polarising in the Wilderness. Bottle versus breast usually becomes a moot point near the beginning of the Wilderness, as your carefully chosen path is dismissed by a child who is happily shovelling in all manner of solids as fast as they can. In first-world cultures, the immunisation and child care debates will roil around for decades to come. Opinions tend to be fixed and debates can rage for weeks with battles fought and lost in the ether. There are long responses in the comments section of blogs or short sharp Twitter skirmishes in a series of 140 character stabs and slashes. Commonalities between opposing opinions are dismissed, overall goals lost, as each individual digs into their personal store of detail to pull out some supporting evidence and the battles rages on.

Once again, it is the strength of your Parenting Gem that will determine your immunity to opinion. An opinion that is held in your heart and is grounded in your own beliefs needs no cheer squad, no clusters of agreeable comments to validate it. Paradoxically, an opinion that is strong is also silent for it is a personal belief; it is not a piece of legislation that requires vast numbers to support it and have it passed as an act of parliament. Voicing an opinion can cause a seismic shift in the dynamic of your herd. Like advice, you learn over time to hold your opinions to yourself and allow those you meet the freedom to hold their own. You have given your voting cards to the children to draw on, and you stay away from those who persist in politicking their beliefs from a soapbox at the crossroads.

GUILT

If advice and opinion make up the river that runs through the Wilderness, guilt is the silt that falls to the bottom; a fine brown sludge that is stirred up into the clear waters at watering holes. It is fine enough to penetrate the pores of your skin and, inadvertently, you drink a little of it each time you are given advice.

The weight of responsibility given to you with the birth of your children increases the further into the parenting journey you venture.

There are societal pressures, family pressures, pressures from your children and there is the pressure you apply to yourself. Guilt pushes down upon you and out from the inside. No matter what choices you make, somewhere someone will have made a comment about it or written an article, a blog-post or even an entire book.

There will be information about all the other choices you could have made, and it only takes a sideways glance at someone who appears to have a happier, healthier Family Beast to have you questioning the choices you have made and the effect they have had. You contemplate the different paths you could have taken and the possible outcomes from those decisions, and before you know it, you are well along the dark path of regret and guilt. The longer you travel down this path, the less sunshine there is. The further you stray from your herd, the deeper you find yourself in a valley filled with confusion and doubt. There are no glowing Parenting Gems to light the way and in the same sense that misery enjoys company, guilt is easy to cultivate and, like most negative things — cockroaches, beetroot stains and head-lice for example — difficult to get rid of. Left to fester, guilt breeds indecision and you are left spinning around with no way out.

The ability to accept that, as a parent, you will make decisions, determine actions and create a family to the best of your ability with the information and materials available at the time, is invaluable. It goes a long way towards alleviating feelings of guilt and accepting your current position, whatever that may be.

Complications do arise when you feel as though something was NOT your decision, that your actions were determined by others and that the definition of your family has been drawn from unwelcome or unhelpful influence. Then, resentment can start to shoot painfully through you like a pinched nerve. Your freedom is hampered and you are forced into some awkward manoeuvres. Guilt and resentment will exhaust you in a time when your energy is a precious resource. It will dehydrate you faster than a jumbo pack of salt and vinegar chips and, in order to slake your thirst, you will return to the river of advice again and again. But it is not advice that will lessen your guilt — it is your acceptance that what has passed cannot be changed, and what is to come will be dealt with as best you can. You cannot return and redo mistakes that are only apparent in hindsight.

Your choices are yours and you make them all the time. In parenting, as in life, to surrender and be blown around by the prevailing winds is as much a decision as putting your head down and striding into a storm with determination. Doing nothing is a choice; it is not the result of indecision, it is in itself a decision. Letting somebody else make the choice for you is actually your choice — you have chosen to hand over the reins. All through the Wilderness you will make compromises big and small because these compromises enable you to move in the direction that you want to go. In hindsight, you may see some choices as misguided, but hindsight is hindsight; it is only helpful if you use it to make a better choice in the future, rather than dwell on a decision made in the past.

In the Wilderness you make decisions for the good of the Family Beast, on behalf of your children, your partner, the guinea pig, and yourself. You make them with all the available resources, and if you make them in a calm and quiet place and not in the heat of the moment, then you usually choose a path that is not too tiring, too long or too difficult for your Beast to travel along.

chapter thirteen

BREAKING CAMP AND MOVING ON

As you approach the end of the Wilderness you are filled with anticipation, a sense of great achievement, and periods of doubt and yearning. It can be almost as confusing as your first few weeks — there is change coming and it appears to be coming fast. But like the lights of an oncoming vehicle on a desert road at night, the initial sighting of the gates out of the Wilderness is deceptive. They are not as close as they appear. In reality, those lights can take months to arrive. The end of the Wilderness is similar. You think you are almost out. The Family Beast is fit, striding out, ears forward, and everyone is fidgeting in excitement. At the back, the Tail is making final preparations and packing away all the things that have no place in the bright new future that lies ahead. The relationship between the Tail and Torso is experiencing a new lease of life. From the babble of chaos, a new harmonious language has emerged and it appears, for the moment, that everyone can both speak and understand this new dialect.

The children have started to move away from the head and, in some instances, can be found down at the tail making beds or washing dishes without breaking anything or building a fort out of pots and pans.

At this point several things can happen and sometimes they all happen at the same time with some mixed results, like a choose your own adventure;

Your Family Beast is trotting along happily. Everyone is out at a friend's place and you suddenly realise that you and your partner are at home. At the same time. Alone. But together.

You:

a) Accidentally launch into an argument of epic proportions where both parties get to pull out just about every lump of discontent, unease and general frustration and hurl them around like medieval flails.

b) Fall into the family bed and use it like it hasn't been used since you realised with your first baby that co-sleeping was the only way anybody was getting any sleep at all.

c) Both of the above (usually, but not necessarily, in chronological order).

Because of the suddenly empty house and the unexpectedness of the opportunity, certain precautions may be overlooked. It may transpire that it was not actually your time to leave the Wilderness; that actually you have to go back to the beginning and start again, with a new member at the head of your Beast. The same journey, but different. (Please turn back to page one now.)

But if it is your time to leave the Wilderness you might be confronted by feelings of sudden loss. It can be devastating, or just feel like a momentary misplacement. What have you lost? You. You have lost your former self and you can't for the life of you remember where you put it.

You know where the missing puzzle piece is, the car keys and the sports uniform. You know the date of the end-of-year school concert and the cat's next worm tablet. You know exactly where you have put everybody else and all their needs. But where, oh where, did you put yourself?

You realise you packed yourself into a box somewhere at the beginning of the journey. You thought it was only for a short time, a few months maybe. But now, years later, you have a dim recollection of madly tossing out a whole lot of stuff you thought you would never need again and maybe that box went out as well. Or did it end up on the council clear-up pile four summers ago? You start to panic, rifling through cupboards, garages, attics and lofts, and in desperation under the sofa, the dress-up basket, behind the bookshelf and in the Everything Drawer, where you are momentarily distracted by the rediscovery of your Parenting Gem, gently glowing at the back surrounded by spare bolts, rubber bands and broken hair-clips.

After weeks of searching, you finally give up and decide that you are just going to have to reconstruct yourself from memory. Of course the first question is, what exactly are you going to construct yourself out of? Clay, hand-dyed yarn and a bamboo crochet hook? Steel or the lump of dried-out brownish play dough from under the five-year-old's bed? And once you finally decide on your media, you suddenly wonder if you really want the old you back at all? Thinking about it, who were you when you packed you away? Were you the kind of person who could stare down the most imposing mother-in-law on the issue of table manners for 18-month-olds? Manage a house full of children with chicken pox while your partner was away on a three-week manufacturing tour of a politically unstable Middle Eastern country? Would you have glared defiantly at the supermarket manager as your children happily ripped open a handful of chocolate bars and left them on the floor to be stepped on? Would you have told the store manager to put the damn chocolate out of reach of children if they didn't want that to happen? Would you? Would you volunteer to have 12 under-fives for a drop-off birthday party, confident that the house, its contents and you would survive? Were you the kind of person who could, at a moment's notice find someone at 2 am to mind a colicky baby and a distraught six-year-old, while you jumped into the farm ute and sped two hours to the local hospital with a three-year-old with a raging temperature and an alarming rattling cough? When greeted by a battle-axe of a nurse, who takes one look at the child and declares, 'There is nothing wrong that couldn't have waited until 9 am when the doctor is on duty,' would you have slunk back home or stood your ground and demanded that the bloody doctor be called NOW? Well? Were you?

Do you really want to be that person again? Or are you now a stronger and braver version of your old self?

The future is new and bright and shiny and you have been in the Wilderness for so long, everyone has forgotten who you were anyway. You realise this is a moment of pure possibility and you can become anyone now. You can reinvent yourself, go to university, change careers, start a career, volunteer for a charity. Suddenly you find yourself in deep conversation with your child about all the things you could do. 'Astronaut!' he yells helpfully. 'Princess! Zoo Keeper! Monster Truck!' You are on a roll and suddenly the future is wide open. The dried-out brown play dough goes into the bin with a Michael Jordan-esque flourish and you forget all about your old self and start to build a brand new you from scratch, using coloured pencils and the energy generated by a the imagination of an enthusiastic five-year-old.

Leaving the Wilderness can, in the end, be a very quick transition — one minute you are in the thick of it then, without warning, you are out of it. For such a longed-for moment, it can be quietly underwhelming — an anti-climax. You may have considered all the options, made lists of all the things you want to do before the children start school and another list of all the things you want to do afterwards. Some of you may already have started — a bit of study here, some part-time work there, in a steady progression towards the day when you can step back into the Holy Grail of parenting — your old life. For some of us this involves holding onto the ties of our past careers, for others it can be seen as a great opportunity for re-invention. None of us really expect it to be a simple, smooth transition, but we do hope that some of the camaraderie of the Wilderness will flow over into the actual world. For some this is the case and for others the reality of job hunting, CV's and interviews is daunting.

The other thing you don't really expect is how little time you actually have once you have dropped the children at school, travelled to your place of study or work and sat down at your desks. Suddenly you notice that it is fifteen minutes past the time you were supposed to leave to go and collect everyone again.

Parents, in particular mothers, who are returning to work are one of the most underestimated, maligned groups of people in the workforce. Pitifully grateful for any employment at all, mothers returning to the workforce will often accept reduced roles, responsibilities, conditions, and pay.

It is possible that if every parent wishing to return to the workforce were offered the opportunity to work in the public service for twelve months to 're-skill', this country would, like an F1 race car, go from a standstill to over 100 kilometres per hour, leaving bureaucrats spinning like tops for years to come. Like an undiscovered, untapped and renewable energy source, mothers returning to the workforce are NONE of the following:

➤ distracted

➤ unfocused

➤ undedicated

➤ unreliable

➤ unwilling.

They are, however — after years and years of working in adverse conditions — some of the most efficient, focused and dedicated employees around. They have limited time and they are very aware of this, and know how to get enormous amounts of work done efficiently. They don't chit-chat at the water cooler, procrastinate or leave things unfinished. Their interior stopwatch is racing, not against time, but against circumstance. They are acutely aware that at any moment the school can ring to let them know their youngest child is in sick-bay with suspected chicken pox. There is no option for delay, rescheduling or delegating. They must be absolutely and completely on top of everything they have been tasked with and one step ahead on the things they know are coming their way. It is almost understandable that some middle-aged, middle-manager types might find this effectiveness somewhat threatening.

If you study, you are the annoying mature-age student who hands in assignments prior to deadline and manages your time according to your family schedule rather than your university timetable. You know what prepared actually means, and the full ramifications of what not being prepared will be. A fail on an assignment will barely register as a blip on the radar if you miss the six-year-old's end of term violin recital.

As you near the end of the Wilderness, you will notice that while previously 80 percent of your time has been spent in a physical and emotional endurance test, the end of the Wilderness signifies a change in the kind of efforts required. Your offspring have become competent communicators and have started to develop a sense of reason. There is a shift toward more intellectual challenges. Everyone is a little more familiar with each other — and not necessarily in a good way. There are buttons, and they are being pushed for all they are worth. The bigger and redder the button, the more likely it is to be pushed. You try, as the mature adult, to keep all your buttons hidden, but your offspring are older, stronger, smarter, and faster than ever before. Your mental capacity, after years of neglect, is suddenly getting a workout that leaves you aching and exhausted in an entirely different way. You secretly wonder if you are even remotely qualified for what lies beyond the Wilderness.

You have about five-years' worth of chores on your list of things to do next time you don't have children with you. The list looks like this:

- Have mole removed (already done by small child with a sharp fingernail).

- Book facial.

- Call for results of tests regarding Asperger's. (For goodness sake, which child was that for?)

- Four-month post-natal check-up (dated five years ago).

➤ Pap smear (x 6).

➤ Send flowers. (An engagement, an apology, a birth, a death? You have no idea who or what for.)

You drop everybody off for their first day of school. You take a few moments to brush down your Family Beast and fondly farewell him. In fact you are almost tearful as he canters around a corner and out of sight. Slipping through the gates marked ENTER HERE, you head off to Civilisation, confident that you finally have your life back…

AN AFTERWORD FROM BEYOND THE WILDERNESS

It's been a long week. You have packed school lunches, consoled a broken heart (a 'Sammy says she's not friends with me any more' type of heartbreak, not teenage heartbreak or actual heartbreak, but no less devastating apparently). You have cleaned the house properly, started a part-time job, volunteered for the school canteen, and the weekend sports roster. After finally bribing everyone with things you neither have nor can afford, you managed to get everyone's homework done (The ambiguity is intentional). You have tidied the kitchen, pre-prepared for a work meeting, packed tomorrow's backpacks and thrown a load of dirty clothes in the wash.

Returning from the laundry you are startled to find your Family Beast standing in the middle of the room. He's dishevelled, dusty and has twigs stuck to his fur. You stare at each other in amazement, then you recognise the wild look in his eyes. It is the look of someone who *thought* they had some freedom to roll in the grass, to cavort with their own kind, to roam with no obligation or timetable; the look of someone who realises that actually that won't be happening just yet and everyone had better just get used to it.

Wearily, you climb aboard his warm solid back and you both sigh, resigned to your fate, and the next leg of the journey…

CAMILLE BLYTH is an author and mother. *The Wilderness Years* is her first book. She lives in Sydney, surrounded by pink glitter, empty lunch-boxes and chickens. Her Wilderness Years are over but she knows she's not out of the woods yet.

Printed in Great Britain
by Amazon.co.uk, Ltd.,
Marston Gate.